Effective Teaching Styles

Elisabeth Hayes, *Editor*
Syracuse University

NEW DIRECTIONS FOR CONTINUING EDUCATION

RALPH G. BROCKETT, *Editor-in-Chief*
University of Tennessee, Knoxville

ALAN B. KNOX, *Consulting Editor*
University of Wisconsin

Number 43, Fall 1989

Paperback sourcebooks in
The Jossey-Bass Higher Education Series

Jossey-Bass Inc., Publishers
San Francisco • Oxford

Elisabeth Hayes (ed.).
Effective Teaching Styles.
New Directions for Continuing Education, no. 43.
San Francisco: Jossey-Bass, 1989.

New Directions for Continuing Education
Ralph G. Brockett, *Editor-in-Chief*
Alan B. Knox, *Consulting Editor*

New Directions for Continuing Education is published quarterly
by Jossey-Bass Inc., Publishers (publication number USPS 493-930).
Second-class postage paid at San Francisco, California, and at
additional mailing offices. POSTMASTER: Send address changes to
Jossey-Bass Inc., Publishers, 350 Sansome Street, San Francisco,
California 94104.

Editorial correspondence should be sent to the Editor-in-Chief,
Ralph G. Brockett, Dept. of Technological and Adult Education,
University of Tennessee, 402 Claxton Addition, Knoxville, Tennessee
37996-3400.

Library of Congress Catalog Card Number LC 85-644750

International Standard Serial Number ISSN 0195-2242

International Standard Book Number ISBN 1-55542-840-1

Cover art by WILLI BAUM

Manufactured in the United States of America. Printed on acid-free paper.

Ordering Information

The paperback sourcebooks listed below are published quarterly and can be ordered either by subscription or single copy.

Subscriptions cost $56.00 per year for institutions, agencies, and libraries. Individuals can subscribe at the special rate of $42.00 per year *if payment is by personal check.* (Note that the full rate of $56.00 applies if payment is by institutional check, even if the subscription is designated for an individual.) Standing orders are accepted.

Single copies are available at $12.95 when payment accompanies order. (California, New Jersey, New York, and Washington, D.C., residents please include appropriate sales tax.) For billed orders, cost per copy is $12.95 plus postage and handling.

Substantial discounts are offered to organizations and individuals wishing to purchase bulk quantities of Jossey-Bass sourcebooks. Please inquire.

Please note that these prices are for the calendar year 1989 and are subject to change without notice. Also, some titles may be out of print and therefore not available for sale.

To ensure correct and prompt delivery, all orders must give either the *name of an individual* or an *official purchase order number.* Please submit your order as follows:

Subscriptions: specify series and year subscription is to begin.
Single Copies: specify sourcebook code (such as, CE1) and first two words of title.

Mail all orders to:
Jossey-Bass Inc., Publishers
350 Sansome Street
San Francisco, California 94104

New Directions for Continuing Education Series
Ralph G. Brockett, *Editor-in-Chief*
Alan B. Knox, *Consulting Editor*

CE1   *Enhancing Proficiencies of Continuing Educators,* Alan B. Knox
CE2   *Programming for Adults Facing Mid-Life Change,* Alan B. Knox
CE3   *Assessing the Impact of Continuing Education,* Alan B. Knox

Contents

Editor's Notes

Effective teaching style is a subject of perennial interest in continuing education. The rapidly changing context of continuing education in modern society requires adult educators to continually reassess their teaching practices to meet new needs and situations. For example, as a result of efforts to make education accessible to more adult learners, new instructional formats are being adopted in many settings. The nature of the adult learner is changing as well, as programs seek to serve greater numbers of students with diverse educational, cultural, and socioeconomic backgrounds.

The complex and dynamic nature of the teaching process itself continues to make it difficult or impossible to isolate essential characteristics and skills of the effective teacher. Research and practical experience suggest that good teaching depends on a combination of personal traits, attitudes, and knowledge as well as the ability to select and use appropriate instructional methods and techniques. The term *teaching style* has been used to describe this elusive mixture of qualities that characterize individual approaches to teaching. Teaching style is not a new concept: it has been the focus of theorizing and research for years. However, as Gary J. Conti points out in Chapter One, a problem that continues to plague discussions of teaching style is lack of a clear definition of the concept. There is disagreement over the elements that determine teaching style and the relative contribution of each element to the effectiveness of different styles. While the authors in this volume vary somewhat in their conception of teaching style, a common theme is that the effectiveness of any style is dependent on multiple factors and that teachers can and should be flexible in their approaches to instruction.

There are no easy answers to the question of what teaching style is best in any given situation. Tom (1984, p. 72) suggests that the effective teacher is "able to conceive of his or her teaching in purposeful terms, analyze a particular teaching problem, choose a teaching approach that seems appropriate to the problem, attempt the approach, judge the results in relation to the original purpose, and reconsider either the teaching approach or the original purpose." Adopting this perspective, we can say that the most important skill for teachers ultimately may not be expertise with particular methods as much as it is the ability to engage in a process of critical reflection on the process and outcomes of instruction in relation to the demands of a particular context and an explicit set of values.

The chapters in this volume are intended to assist continuing educators in this process of critical reflection. Topics have been selected from a

1

variety of areas important for teachers of adults in a wide range of continuing education programs. The first two chapters stress the priority of teacher self-understanding as an initial step in developing appropriate teaching styles. In Chapter One, Gary J. Conti describes a means for teachers to gain more insight about elements of their own teaching style and describes research that explores the effectiveness of various styles given different student and contextual variables. In Chapter Two, Jerold W. Apps presents an approach that teachers can use to clarify the values and assumptions that underlie their instructional practices.

In the next chapters, the focus shifts to the potential significance of various aspects of the teaching-learning situation. In Chapter Three, L. Adrianne Bonham discusses learning style as a factor to consider in selecting appropriate teaching strategies. Barbara M. Florini provides an overview of new communications technology in Chapter Four and identifies ways to successfully integrate these new resources into the instructional process. Chapter Five explores the implications of current perspectives on women as learners and describes feminist pedagogy as an alternative instructional model.

The last chapters pull together varied elements and ideas. Gordon G. Darkenwald introduces the concept of classroom social environment in Chapter Six and describes the role of the teacher in shaping an optimal environment for adult learners. Daniel D. Pratt provides an overview in Chapter Seven of several views of teacher competence, suggesting that multiple perspectives may be a valuable means to broaden our understanding of effective teaching. The final chapter identifies resources to further assist both beginning and experienced teachers in efforts to enhance their instructional practices with adult students.

Elisabeth Hayes
Editor

Reference

Tom, A. *Teaching as a Moral Craft.* New York: Longman, 1984.

Elisabeth Hayes is assistant professor of adult education at Syracuse University. Her experience as a teacher of adults ranges from adult basic education to graduate education for adult educators. She currently conducts workshops and teaches courses on adult learning and teaching.

Assessing Teaching Style in Continuing Education

Gary J. Conti

The teaching-learning transaction is a dynamic venture in which both the teacher and learner are active participants. While much attention in adult education has focused on the learner side of this transaction, it is difficult to dispute Knowles's (1970, p. 41) long-standing assertion that "the behavior of the teacher probably influences the character of the learning climate more than any other single factor." A growing body of research is developing that supports the beliefs of most who have taught adults that the way the teacher approaches the learning situation makes a difference in the way students learn. The overall traits and qualities that a teacher displays in the classroom and that are consistent for various situations can be described as *teaching style*. A knowledge of teaching style can make a difference in how teachers organize their classroom, how they deal with learners, and how well their students do in learning the content of the continuing education class.

Although there has been a great deal of interest among educators about the concept of teaching style during the past decade, there has been very little agreement about what actually constitutes teaching style. Most who discuss the concept avoid defining teaching style. Instead, they tend to talk about the elements that make up a teacher's style. Many focus on teaching style as an external teacher characteristic that

E. R. Hayes (ed.). *Effective Teaching Styles.*
New Directions for Continuing Education, no. 43. San Francisco: Jossey-Bass, Fall 1989.

can be manipulated in reaction to student behaviors. Some in this group hold that teaching style is related to how the teacher learned but that it can be modified if the instructor understands how to respond to varied student learning styles (Dunn and Dunn, 1979). Others view teaching style as a set of models from which various teacher behaviors can be selected based upon the types of student outcomes that are desired (Ellis, 1979). Still others link teaching style with learning style. This group ranges from those who narrowly restrict their considerations of learning style to cognitive style (Kuchinskas, 1979) to those who believe that "each dimension (of teaching style) is directly comparable to an equivalent dimension on Learning Styles" (Canfield and Canfield, 1976, p. 1).

Those who support this concept of teaching style as a student-driven phenomenon have two common concerns. First, much of their attention is directed toward seeking the best possible match between learning styles and teaching styles. Second, they tend to equate teaching style with teaching methods and strategies. A better knowledge of teaching style is sought so that style, methods, or strategies can be adjusted to better meet the needs of the learners.

An alternative view conceptualizes teaching style as defined by the internal qualities of the teacher that affect classroom behaviors. The teacher enters the teaching-learning transaction with a definite set of values (Brookfield, 1986). These values influence the teacher's beliefs about such things as the nature of the learner, the purpose of the curriculum, and the role of the teacher (Darkenwald and Merriam, 1982). While a teacher may vary teaching techniques from day to day or from activity to activity in order to accomplish specific learning goals for a specific content area or situation, the beliefs remain relatively stable over the period in which a teacher interacts with a group of learners. The philosophical beliefs are translated into action in the classroom through the teacher's individual teaching style.

Thus, in this perspective, teaching style is differentiated from methods (Fischer and Fischer, 1979). Instead, teaching style might best be viewed as a range of behaviors in which the teacher can operate comfortably according to a certain value system. Specific contexts and learning materials require certain kinds of responses. While personal philosophy provides an overall basis for decisions about appropriate actions, the teacher's behavior will vary in addressing each of these unique classroom situations. The amount of this variance will be limited by tenets of the teacher's educational philosophy and by the strength to which the teacher adheres to that educational philosophy. The way in which the teacher consistently functions within this range defines the teacher's teaching style.

Teaching Style in Adult Education

While a number of ways exist to conceptualize teaching style in this more global manner, much theory and research suggests that there are two fundamental teaching styles: a responsive, collaborative, learner-centered mode and a controlling, teacher-centered mode. A large portion of the literature in the field of adult education supports a collaborative mode as the most effective and appropriate style for teaching adults. Several common themes supporting the collaborative mode can be traced from seminal works in the field by such authors as Eduard Lindeman ([1926] 1961) to current award-winning books by such authors as Stephen Brookfield (1986) and Laurent Daloz (1987). Collectively, these works point out that the key word for working successfully with adults is *participation.* Ideally the learner should be an active participant in a learning activity that is a cooperative venture. One way to engage learners in these activities is through the use of their experience. Adults have a rich reservoir of experiences that are intense in scope and that provide them with a background for evaluating new situations, relationships, and content. Continuing education activities can provide either a mechanism for gaining a better understanding of their experiences or an opportunity to apply their experiences to new learning.

To a great extent, adults learn about things to solve the particular problems they face in life. By being active in the learning process and by relating their experiences to the problem under study, they are able to take responsibility for their own learning. To solve problems, adults must have more than knowledge. In terms of educational objectives (Bloom, Krathwohl, and Masia, 1973), they must be able to apply, analyze, synthesize, and evaluate the material being learned. These higher-level cognitive skills can only be achieved by actively involving the learner in the learning process.

The role of the teacher in this process is to organize and maintain an environment that facilitates student learning. The teacher brings ideas, values, and experiences to the learning transaction and is charged with the task of drawing ideas, opinions, and values out of learners. In this transaction, teacher and learners are mutual partners. Thus, the collaborative mode as professed in the adult education literature is a learner-centered approach to education. The emphases are upon what the learner is doing and upon how the teacher is facilitating that process. The curriculum is problem centered, and the entire process is very democratic.

Although the adult education literature supports the collaborative mode as the most appropriate way to teach adults, many adult educators do not totally accept or utilize this approach. While these major tenets are based upon "at least three reasonably cogent foundations: informed professional opinion; philosophical assumptions associated with humanistic psychology and progressive education; and a growing body of research and theory on adult learning, development, and socialization" (Beder and Darkenwald, 1982, p. 143), they are general in nature and do not take into consideration the unique situations in which many adult educators find themselves. Do these findings apply equally to adult educators who are conducting training in business and industry, to those who are doing continuing professional education, or to teachers who are instructing in the military?

They probably do not, because the teaching situation is influenced by four interacting variables: the nature of the learner, the teacher, the situation, and the content. Both the learners and the teacher have different needs and styles. Situational factors, such as the mission of the sponsoring agency, the available facilities, and the allotted time, regulate what can be done. Finally, different types of content require different strategies for teaching them effectively. These four elements interact in different ways and in different proportions for each teaching situation. Consequently, teachers cannot blindly accept the major tenets of the literature. Instead, they must enhance their self-knowledge so that they can be proactive in interacting with the other three variables. An important step in understanding themselves as teachers is assessing their personal teaching style.

Assessing Teaching Style

One instrument that has been used widely to assess teaching style in adult education is the Principles of Adult Learning Scale (PALS). This forty-four-item instrument uses a modified Likert scale (see Figure 1), it can be completed in less than fifteen minutes, and it can be self-scored. To assess their style, teachers indicate the frequency with which they practice the actions described in the items. These items represent actual classroom behaviors. The PALS score is determined by adding the value for each response (see Figure 2).

The PALS is based upon principles that are advanced in the adult education literature. The total score on the PALS gives an indication of the teacher's overall preference for a learner-centered or teacher-centered teaching style in an adult education setting. In the learner-centered approach, the authority for curriculum formation is shared by the learner and the teacher. In the teacher-centered approach, authority resides with the teacher. High scores on the PALS reflect a learner-centered approach to the teaching-learning transaction. Low scores on PALS reflect a preference for the teacher-centered approach. Scores near the mean of 146 for the instrument indicate a combination of teaching behaviors that draws elements from both the learner-centered and the teacher-centered

Figure 1. Principles of Adult Learning Scale (PALS)

Directions: The following survey contains several things that a teacher of adults might do in a classroom. You may personally find some of them desirable and find others undesirable. For each item please respond to the way you most frequently practice the action described in the item. Your choices are Always, Almost Always, Often, Seldom, Almost Never, and Never. On your answer sheet, circle 0 if you always do the event; circle number 1 if you almost always do the event; circle number 2 if you often do the event; circle number 3 if you seldom do the event; circle number 4 if you almost never do the event; and circle number 5 if you never do the event. If the item *does not apply* to you, circle number 5 for never.

Always	Almost Always	Often	Seldom	Almost Never	Never
0	1	2	3	4	5

1. I allow students to participate in developing the criteria for evaluating their performance in class.
2. I use disciplinary action when it is needed.
3. I allow older students more time to complete assignments when they need it.
4. I encourage students to adopt middle class values.
5. I help students diagnose the gaps between their goals and their present level of performance.
6. I provide knowledge rather than serve as a resource person.
7. I stick to the instructional objectives that I write at the beginning of a program.
8. I participate in the informal counseling of students.
9. I use lecturing as the best method for presenting my subject material to adult students.
10. I arrange the classroom so that it is easy for students to interact.
11. I determine the educational objectives for each of my students.
12. I plan units which differ as widely as possible from my students' socio-economic backgrounds.
13. I get a student to motivate himself/herself by confronting him/her in the presence of classmates during group discussions.
14. I plan learning episodes to take into account my students' prior experiences.
15. I allow students to participate in making decisions about the topics that will be covered in class.
16. I use one basic teaching method because I have found that most adults have a similar style of learning.
17. I use different techniques depending on the students being taught.
18. I encourage dialogue among my students.
19. I use written tests to assess the degree of academic growth rather than to indicate new directions for learning.
20. I utilize the many competencies that most adults already possess to achieve educational objectives.
21. I use what history has proven that adults need to learn as my chief criteria for planning learning episodes.
22. I accept errors as a natural part of the learning process.
23. I have individual conferences to help students identify their educational needs.

Figure 1. *(continued)*

24. I let each student work at his/her own rate regardless of the amount of time it takes him/her to learn a new concept.
25. I help my students develop short-range as well as long-range objectives.
26. I maintain a well disciplined classroom to reduce interferences to learning.
27. I avoid discussion of controversial subjects that involve value judgments.
28. I allow my students to take periodic breaks during class.
29. I use methods that foster quiet, productive desk-work.
30. I use tests as my chief method of evaluating students.
31. I plan activities that will encourage each student's growth from dependence on others to greater independence.
32. I gear my instructional objectives to match the individual abilities and needs of the students.
33. I avoid issues that relate to the student's concept of himself/herself.
34. I encourage my students to ask questions about the nature of their society.
35. I allow a student's motives for participating in continuing education to be a major determinant in the planning of learning objectives.
36. I have my students identify their own problems that need to be solved.
37. I give all students in my class the same assignment on a given topic.
38. I use materials that were originally designed for students in elementary and secondary schools.
39. I organize adult learning episodes according to the problems that my students encounter in everyday life.
40. I measure a student's long-term educational growth by comparing his/her total achievement in class to his/her expected performance as measured by national norms from standardized tests.
41. I encourage competition among my students.
42. I use different materials with different students.
43. I help students relate new learning to their prior experiences.
44. I teach units about problems of everyday living.

approaches. Thus, the PALS score indicates the teacher's overall teaching style, the strength of the support for this style, and the degree to which the teacher accepts the general ideas in the mainstream adult education literature.

The overall PALS score can be broken down into seven factors. While the overall score indicates the teacher's general style, the factor scores identify specific elements that make up this style. The factor titles reflect support of the collaborative mode. High scores on each factor represent support of the concept implied in the factor title; low scores indicate support of the opposite concept. For example, a high score on factor 6 indicates a teaching style that gives learners many choices in how to achieve learning goals once the curriculum has been set and that encourages the students to take responsibility for their learning activities. A low score on factor 6 indicates a style in which the teacher defines and directs the exact learning activities that each student undertakes to accomplish the learning goals. Factor scores are calculated by adding the responses for each item in the factor (see Figure 2).

Figure 2. PALS Scoring

Positive Items

Items number 1, 3, 5, 8, 10, 14, 15, 17, 18, 20, 22, 23, 24, 25, 28, 31, 32, 34, 35, 36, 39, 42, 43, and 44 are positive items. For positive items, the following values are assigned: Always = 5, Almost Always = 4, Often = 3, Seldom = 2, Almost Never = 1, and Never = 0.

Negative Items

Items number 2, 4, 6, 7, 9, 11, 12, 13, 16, 19, 21, 26, 27, 29, 30, 33, 37, 38, 40, and 41 are negative items. For negative items, the following values are assigned: Always = 0, Almost Always = 1, Often = 2, Seldom = 3, Almost Never = 4, and Never = 5.

Missing Items

Omitted items are assigned a neutral value of 2.5.

Factors

Factor 1 (learner-centered activities)
  contains items 2, 4, 11, 12, 13, 16, 19, 21, 29, 30, 38, and 40.

Factor 2 (personalizing instruction)
  contains items 3, 9, 17, 24, 32, 35, 37, 41, and 42.

Factor 3 (relating to experience)
  contains items 14, 31, 34, 39, 43, and 44.

Factor 4 (assessing student needs)
  contains items 5, 8, 23, and 25.

Factor 5 (climate building)
  contains items 18, 20, 22, and 28.

Factor 6 (participation in the learning process)
  contains items 1, 10, 15, and 36.

Factor 7 (flexibility for personal development)
  contains items 6, 7, 26, 27, and 33.

Computing Scores

An individual's total score on the instrument is calculated by summing the value of the responses to all items. Factor scores are calculated by summing the value of the responses for each item in the factor.

Factor Score Values

Factor	Mean	Standard Deviation
1	38	8.3
2	31	6.8
3	21	4.9
4	14	3.6
5	16	3.0
6	13	3.5
7	13	3.9

Factor 1 is Learner-Centered Activities. This factor consists of twelve negative items in the scale. Low scores on this factor indicate support for the use of formal testing and for the use of standardized tests as a means of comparing learners to established standards. Low scores also express an acceptance of traditional middle-class values and a belief that most learners have a common style for learning. They also indicate a desire for a quiet, orderly classroom in which the teacher determines the learning objectives for each student. High scores indicate an emphasis on informal evaluation techniques, on classroom behaviors that encourage students to take initiating actions, and on having students take responsibility for their own learning.

Factor 2 is Personalizing Instruction. It contains six positive items and three negative items. High scores indicate a preference for designing the learning situation to fit the individual needs of each student. Self-paced learning is encouraged. A variety of methods, materials, and assignments is used. Learning objectives are designed to fit individual motives and abilities. Cooperation rather than competition is encouraged.

Factor 3 is Relating to Experience. It consists of six positive items. High scores indicate a recognition of the importance of a student's prior experiences as an aid for learning. Learning activities are made relevant by organizing them according to problems the students face in everyday life. In this way, students are encouraged to ask basic questions about the nature of their society. It is believed that such a process fosters a student's growth from dependence on others to greater independence.

Factor 4 is Assessing Student Needs. It is made up of four positive items. High scores indicate a desire for finding out what each student wants and needs to know. This assessment is achieved through the use of individual conferences and much informal counseling. Students are involved in diagnosing gaps in their present level of knowledge and skills and in developing objectives for addressing these learning needs.

Factor 5 is Climate Building. It contains four positive items. High scores reflect an attempt to establish a learning climate that is both physically and psychologically comfortable for the learners. Students are encouraged to practice self-control by taking periodic breaks and by interacting with other students. Educational barriers are reduced by utilizing the numerous competencies that adults already possess as part of the learning process. Errors are accepted as a natural and beneficial part of learning. Students are encouraged to take risks, and failures serve as feedback to direct future learning.

Factor 6 is Participation in the Learning Process. It contains four positive items. This factor addresses the amount of involvement that the student has in determining the nature and evaluation of the content material. High scores indicate support for allowing students to identify the problems that they wish to solve and to participate in deciding the topics that will be covered in class. Likewise, students are involved in developing the criteria for evaluation of classroom performance.

Factor 7 is Flexibility for Personal Development. It contains five negative items. Low scores indicate a view of the teacher as a provider of knowledge rather than as a facilitator. Once developed, educational objectives remain unchanged regardless of the divergent needs that might arise. A well-disciplined classroom is maintained, and the discussion of controversial subjects that involve value judgments or of issues that relate to the student's self-concept is avoided.

In assessing teaching style with PALS, a teacher should look for several things. First, the overall score should be calculated. Does this total score seem to fit the teacher's self-image? Does the score indicate a strong degree of support of a certain teaching style? Is this score shocking or satisfying? Second, the factor scores should be determined. Are all the factor scores congruent with the overall score? Teachers who score near the mean for PALS often have one or two factor scores that are significantly different from the others. Why are these scores different? What is the teacher doing in the classroom that causes these conflicts? Third, the item values within the individual factors should be reviewed to identify specific items that received responses that were radically different from the responses to other items in this factor. Why were these items so different? By reviewing the PALS scores in such a manner, teachers can better understand the elements that cause them to act the way they do in the classroom.

Relationships Between Teaching Style and Learning

In addition to being a tool for instructors' personal assessment of teaching style, the PALS has been used in numerous research studies. Several of these studies have focused on describing teaching practices in various areas of continuing education. Others have explored the relationships between teaching style and student outcomes. Collectively, these studies are beginning to indicate a pattern in the influence of teaching style on student learning.

The first research using the PALS that related teaching style to student learning was conducted with adult basic education students in South Texas (Conti, 1985). In this study, the teaching style of twenty-nine part-time instructors was measured with the PALS, and their teaching style was compared with students' achievement in the program. Statistical evidence indicated that the teacher's style had a significant influence on the amount of the students' academic gain. However, these gains were not consistent with the general adult education literature; that is, the students of the teachers who practiced the collaborative, learner-centered mode did not always have the highest degree of achievement. Instead, the influence of teaching style differed according to the type of classes in the program. In the classes preparing students to take the General Educational Development (GED) test, the teacher-centered approach was most effective; this finding seemed to contradict the conventional wisdom in the adult education literature that the collaborative mode is generally the most effective means for teaching adults. However, in the English-as-a-Second-Language (ESL) and the basic-level classes, the findings were consistent with the general adult education literature. Here, the learner-centered approach led to the most learning.

These findings indicated that the effectiveness of a teaching style is related to other factors. While teaching style definitely affects learning, some styles are more appropriate in certain situations than others. In this study, potentially important situational factors included differences in the goals of the learners. Learners in GED classes are highly motivated to pass the official GED test. Their lack of high school certification poses a barrier in their lives that prevents them from getting a job, securing a job promotion, or meeting entry requirements for an educational program. Passing the GED test can eliminate this barrier and allow them to move on to goals and opportunities in their lives. Therefore, they typically want to pass this test as quickly as possible, and the teacher is just the person to help them do this. Since the teacher should be familiar with this standardized exam and since the learner has no control over the testing conditions, a teacher-centered approach is an effective way for many learners to get what they need from the educational situation.

However, the motivation for basic-level and ESL students may be very different. These students have lacked basic reading, writing, math, and language skills for all their lives. Now that they have either entered school for the first time or returned to school, they may have more of an intrinsic desire to learn. They are not pursuing skills that prepare them to take a standardized test; rather, they are seeking skills to overcome lifelong academic deficiencies that can be related to their self-concept. The risk taking that is inherent in this process requires a supportive environment with an accepting teacher. A learner-centered approach provides a learning situation in which the students can deal with personal concerns while they are developing academic skills.

Thus, this first study examined the relationship of teaching style to student achievement and confirmed that the style of the teacher was related to how students learned. However, it also indicated that one teaching style cannot be generically prescribed for all teachers, students, situations, and content. While it showed that teaching style interacted with other variables in the teaching-learning transaction, questions still remained about how individual teachers could estimate the potential effectiveness of their style in a specific situation.

A second study helped to clarify the dilemma for teachers (Conti and Welborn, 1986). Involving eighteen teachers and 256 students, it examined the relationship of teaching style to academic achievement for allied health professionals taking credit classes in a nontraditional format, such as evening courses, weekend classes, and off-campus courses. Like the first study, it found teaching style to be significantly related to student achievement. As the adult education literature suggests, the students of the teachers practicing the learner-centered approach achieved at a level that was higher than the average for the total group. However, students of teachers who had very high scores for practicing the teacher-centered approach also achieved above the average. At the same time, no differences in student motivation, content, or situation were obvious from the design of the study. Thus, while the results supported the use of the collaborative, learner-centered approach as an effective means of teaching adults, it also suggested that a teacher-centered approach can be effective. Still unanswered were questions about when each of these approaches is most effective and how teachers can know if their style is appropriate in their own situation.

A third study in this same general line of inquiry helped to resolve some of these unanswered questions. Conducted at Montana's seven tribal colleges, it involved predominantly Native Americans (Conti and Fellenz, 1988). Tribal colleges are community colleges that are located on Indian reservations and controlled by the Indian tribe. They have the dual function of delivering postsecondary education and of maintaining the cultural heritage of the tribe. Most of the students at these colleges are nontraditional adult learners. By involving all seven colleges in the state, the study was able to go beyond the limited number of teachers involved in the other studies; eighty teachers and their 1,447 students participated in this study. These numbers allowed for a greater distribution of teaching styles. Teaching styles were labeled Moderate, Intermediate, High, Very High, or Extremely High for both the teacher-centered and the learner-centered approach. In contrast to findings from the first two studies, teaching style as indicated by the overall PALS score did not relate to differences in student academic achievement. However, differences in the teachers' scores on the seven factors that compose PALS did have a relationship to student achievement and helped to clarify the findings of the previous studies.

Differences in student achievement were found to be related to differences in orientation of teaching style on six of the seven factors. While there were some variations among individual factors, a general pattern emerged. With the exception of the factor dealing with formal evaluation, an Extremely High orientation toward either a learner-centered approach or a teacher-centered approach on any factor was related to lower levels of student achievement. In contrast, less extreme but still Very High orientations toward either learner-centered or teacher-centered styles on several factors were associated with higher student achievement levels. Thus, while student achievement tended to suffer with the extreme practice of a teaching style, students prospered with the Very High practice of either style.

A notable exception to this general pattern of improved student achievement for teachers with Very High orientations was in the area of assessing student needs. Here, students experiencing a Very High teacher-centered approach achieved significantly below the overall average for all students. The teacher-centered approach relies on striving for accepted norms rather than upon giving a high priority to involving individual students in a personal definition of their learning needs. The lack of achievement revealed in the third study suggests that the teacher-centered approach to needs assessment is not beneficial to adult learners and that those who are otherwise consistently practicing the teacher-centered approach may want to reconceptualize this element of their educational philosophy to better fit adult learners.

The other categories did not reveal a uniform pattern. While a High orientation toward a learner-centered approach on a teaching style factor was also generally associated with greater levels of student achievement, an inconsistent relationship was found between a High teacher-centered orientation on the various factors and student achievement. Intermediate and Moderate orientations toward a teaching style for all factors were generally related to average student achievement. These styles neither greatly helped nor greatly hindered students' academic performance.

Thus, while these results suggest that the learner-centered approach is generally effective, they also indicate that consistency within key teaching style elements may be the most important element in fostering improved student achievement. Teachers who score Very High in either approach are consistently implementing important aspects of a teaching style. Each of their actions supports the others. Students can predict and understand their teacher's behaviors. Students are not surprised constantly and frustrated. Instead, they know what to expect from the teacher and what to do to satisfy the demands of the class. This consistency allows both the teacher and the students to be comfortable in the learning environment.

Consistency does not mean rigidity. Teachers who are extreme in their teaching style orientations do not allow for needed flexibility. Student achievement drops for adult students with such teachers. On the teacher-centered side, an extreme orientation indicates that student needs and input are being ignored. On the learner-centered side, it implies that the teacher is disregarding the student's need for some degree of structure. In either case, the extreme scores indicate teachers who are not able to adjust to student needs.

The scores in the middle ranges refute cries for an eclectic approach to education. Teaching style scores in the Moderate and Intermediate ranges identify teachers who practice behaviors from both approaches. Their average scores may be the result of having a moderate commitment to one overall orientation or to having conflicting scores across the various factors that compose a particular teaching style. In either case, they are not presenting a definitive image to their students. At best, they help students to perform at a mediocre level. At worst, they do not seem to foster below-average student achievement. However, the research indicates that a better approach to teaching that helps students to achieve more is possible.

Conclusion

Over the centuries, much has been written about what goes on in the classroom, and philosophical stances have been developed to explain and defend various classroom actions. Recent research on teaching style indicates that the things that teachers do in the classroom make a difference in how their students learn. Although a learner-centered approach is generally successful with adult learners, it must be applied in a consistent fashion that is not extreme. However, not all teachers are comfortable with this approach or support its underlying assumptions. For them, the consistent application of the teacher-centered approach can be successful and beneficial to their students. However, in using this approach, they may need to reassess the inadequate attention that this approach gives to the universal demand of adult learners for the proper assessment of student learning needs.

As professionals, teachers need to know their own personal teaching philosophy and the degree to which their actions reflect this set of beliefs. An instrument like the PALS can be useful in assessing this teaching style and in identifying any inconsistencies in style. Such an analysis can suggest topics for professional development and areas for personal reflection. Such actions may shift the educational debate from an argument over which style is best to an examination of the internal consistency of each teacher's actions. Such a course holds exciting prospects for the field, for the individual teacher, and, most of all, for improved student learning.

References

Beder, H. W., and Darkenwald, G. G. "Differences Between Teaching Adults and Pre-Adults: Some Propositions and Findings." *Adult Education*, 1982, *32* (3), 142–155.

Bloom, B. S., Krathwohl, D. R., and Masia, B. *Taxonomy of Educational Objectives*. London: Longman, 1973.

16

Brookfield, S. D. *Understanding and Facilitating Adult Learning: A Comprehensive Analysis of Principles and Effective Practices.* San Francisco: Jossey-Bass, 1986.

Canfield, A. A., and Canfield, J. S. *Canfield Instructional Styles Inventory Manual.* Rochester, Minn.: Humanics Media, 1976.

Conti, G. J. "The Relationship Between Teaching Style and Adult Student Learning." *Adult Education Quarterly,* 1985, *35* (4), 220–228.

Conti, G. J., and Fellenz, R. F. "Teaching and Learning Styles and the Native American Learner." In *Proceedings of the 29th Adult Education Research Conference.* Calgary, Alberta: University of Calgary, 1988.

Conti, G. J., and Welborn, R. B. "Teaching-Learning Styles and the Adult Learner." *Lifelong Learning,* 1986, *9* (8), 20–24.

Daloz, L. A. *Effective Teaching and Mentoring: Realizing the Transformational Power of Adult Learning Experiences.* San Francisco: Jossey-Bass, 1987.

Darkenwald, G. G., and Merriam, S. B. *Adult Education: Foundations of Practice.* New York: Harper & Row, 1982.

Dunn, R. S., and Dunn, K. J. "Learning Styles/Teaching Styles: Should They . . . Can They . . . Be Matched?" *Educational Leadership,* 1979, *36,* 238–244.

Ellis, S. S. "Models of Teaching: A Solution to the Teaching Style/Learning Style Dilemma." *Educational Leadership,* 1979, *36,* 274–277.

Fischer, B. B., and Fisher, L. "Styles in Teaching and Learning." *Educational Leadership,* 1979, *36,* 245–254.

Knowles, M. S. *The Modern Practice of Adult Education.* New York: Association Press, 1970.

Kuchinskas, G. "Whose Cognitive Style Makes the Difference?" *Educational Leadership,* 1979, *36,* 269–271.

Lindeman, E. C. *The Meaning of Adult Education.* Montreal: Harvest House, 1961. (Originally published, 1926.)

Gary J. Conti is associate professor of adult education and Kellogg researcher at the Center for Adult Learning Research, Montana State University, Bozeman. He is coeditor of Adult Literacy and Basic Education *and author of the Principles of Adult Learning Scale.*

*Identifying and examining personal beliefs and values can help
teachers of adults improve their performance and change the
way in which they view their roles as teachers.*

Foundations for Effective Teaching

Jerold W. Apps

Identifying and analyzing our foundations as teachers of adults can help
us in several ways. One of the most obvious contributions is simply
knowing the beliefs and values that undergird our thoughts and actions.
As Gary J. Conti points out in Chapter One, these beliefs and values are
directly related to our styles as teachers. Many of us have not taken time
to think systematically about the foundations of our teaching practices.
From time to time, we face decision points as teachers. What is the best
way of presenting this information? In what ways might I use certain
technology? What is the basis for my decision to share this information
but not that?

Knowing our foundations—becoming conscious of what we believe
and value—can help us to make these and similar decisions. We all have
some foundation for what we do. It comes to us from our childhood,
from our schooling, from the community in which we grew up, and
from authority figures with whom we have come in contact. Some dimensions of our foundation may be hidden from us or are, as Bem (1970)
suggests, zero-order beliefs. Zero-order beliefs influence what we do, but
we are not aware that we hold them. The process of examining our
foundations can help us uncover these zero-order beliefs, analyze them,
and make judgments about them.

E. R. Hayes (ed.). *Effective Teaching Styles.*
New Directions for Continuing Education, no. 43. San Francisco: Jossey-Bass, Fall 1989.

The process of analyzing and making judgments about our beliefs and values on the way toward developing a solid foundation for teaching can have other benefits as well. First, such an analysis can help us become aware of what we do as teachers of adults. It can help create for us what Maxine Greene (1978) calls a wide-awakeness—a sensitivity to what we are doing and why we are doing it.

Second, an analysis of foundations helps us consider alternatives— other ways of doing what we do. The process I outline in this chapter suggests that we look at a wide array of alternatives ranging from various ways of thinking about adults as learners to how we view content and technological aids to teaching.

Third, as we begin to analyze what we do as teachers and why we do it, our fundamental beliefs and values begin to emerge. We begin wrestling with deeper questions. As Greene (1978, p. 46) says, "It is far too easy for teachers, like other people, to play their roles and do their jobs without serious consideration of the good and right." Or, as Alan Tom (1984) argues, we must examine the moral dimensions of what we do.

Ultimately, an analysis of our foundations as a teacher can help empower us. We can begin to feel that we are in control of ourselves as teachers and are not dependent on someone to tell us what to do and how to do it. We also can develop a new relationship with specialists. As Wendell Berry (1977, p. 21) says, "that [a person] is dependent upon so many specialists, the beneficiary of so much expert help, can only mean that he is a captive, a potential victim. If he lives by the competence of so many other people, then he lives also by their indulgence; his own will and his own reasons to live are made subordinate to the mere tolerance of everybody else."

A Process for Analysis

Several years ago, I began working on a process that teachers and other adult educators could use in analyzing what they do (Apps, 1985). The process includes three levels of analysis. The first level, which I call *critical analysis,* is where adult educators examine critically what they now do. I suggest that educators should examine definitions—how we define *learning, adult, program,* and so forth; examine slogans—what does "start where the learner is" really mean?; examine the reasoning of statements—does my argument on some particular point make logical sense; examine the assumptions that undergird what we do; and identify and analyze the metaphors that we use to describe ourselves as teachers and the metaphors that we use to describe adult learners and the teaching-learning transaction. I use Scheffler's (1960, p. 48) definition of metaphor: the metaphorical statement indicates "that there is an important analogy between two things, without saying explicitly in what the analogy consists." Later, I will share several examples of metaphors that are commonly used to describe the teacher and the learning process.

In the second phase of the analysis process, which I call the *synoptic phase*, we examine alternative perspectives to our beliefs and values. What does the literature say about adults as learners? What alternative metaphors describe the adult learning process?

The third and final phase in this analysis process is to reassess what we believe and value once we have worked through the critical and synoptic phases. I call this final phase *normative analysis*. I should quickly point out that the process is not a linear one, although it makes some sense to begin with the critical phase. Some people, though, find reading and discussing alternative views (the synoptic phase) helpful in their own critical analysis. And, those who wrestle with the normative phase often find they need more information and are quickly back in the synoptic phase and sometimes back to critical analysis.

Also, the process is a never ending one. In my judgment, teachers of adults, as part of their ongoing growth and development, will often find it necessary to reexamine the foundations of what they do. So, the process continues—perhaps starting at the synoptic phase and then moving back to critical analysis before once more moving to the normative phase or rather systematically beginning with a critical analysis of some new idea, some approach that may have triggered an analysis of basic beliefs.

I suggest that the three phases of the analysis process—critical, synoptic, and normative—should be conducted within the framework described in the next section. I developed the framework, and I have applied it in a variety of adult and continuing education settings (Apps, 1973, 1979, 1985, 1988).

Framework for Analyzing Foundations

As I discuss the framework, I will illustrate the process, focusing particularly on questions that ought to help us get at alternative views of the teaching-learning transaction for teaching adults. I discuss two of the critical analysis processes: analysis of assumptions and analysis of metaphors.

The framework includes four elements: an examination of our beliefs about adults as learners, the aims we have for our teaching, our beliefs about the subject matter of content of our teaching, and our beliefs about teachers and the teaching-learning transaction. We will look at each of these in turn. For each, I will mention questions that may prove helpful as you begin to examine your beliefs and values within each of these areas, and begin to identify and examine your own assumptions. As appropriate, I will mention metaphors that should prove helpful as you begin to identify and examine the metaphors that guide your work.

Beliefs About Adults as Learners. What you believe about human beings, their potential for growth and development, their motivations for learning, the extent to which they have freedom or they are genetically or environmentally influenced affects you as a teacher.

For example, let us look at two teachers operating in similar situations but performing quite differently. I will call them Jane and Steve. Both have about ten years of teaching experience. Both teach noncredit writing courses for their university extension divisions. Jane is teaching a class in article writing to a group ranging in age from twenty-five to sixty-five. The students are seated in rows facing the instructor. On the day of our visit, Jane is using an overhead projector to display excerpts from articles that students had turned in. She stands in front of the class carefully explaining the good and poor points of each excerpt. From time to time, a student asks a question, which Jane takes time to answer carefully and politely.

Jane works from a course syllabus that lists the course objectives in performance terms. That is, upon completion of the course, students will be expected to know and do certain specific tasks related to article writing. The syllabus also includes the topics to be covered during each session, the assignments required, and the readings suggested.

A short time later, we visit Steve's article writing class. The students also appear to range in age from about twenty-five to sixty-five. When we enter Steve's classroom, we see the students working in groups of three. We ask Steve what they are doing. He responds, "They are evaluating excerpts from articles that they had previously turned in." Steve goes on to explain that he developed a set of criteria for evaluating articles, and he has students participate in the evaluation process. When the evaluations are discussed, he adds his comments to those offered by the students.

Steve uses a syllabus that suggests assignments and appropriate readings. But no assignments are required. He explains that he has several objectives for the class, which he includes in the syllabus, but the class members also offer suggestions as to what they want to receive from the experience. So, ultimately, the objectives are a combination of student and teacher objectives.

I could go on at length about these two instructors, but space prohibits it. Are you more like Steve, or are you more like Jane? What assumptions about adults as learners guide each of them?

I will mention a few; I am sure you can add others. Jane assumes, at least in this class, that she knows better than the students what good writing is. She also assumes that students expect her to be in charge of the class. In contrast, Steve assumes that students in a writing class can learn to evaluate their own and their peers' writing. He also assumes that students want to be involved in a writing class and that they do not expect him to dominate the class.

You can ask a series of questions that help to get at the assumptions in your own teaching situations. You can ask questions about relationships. How do you see human beings relating to the natural environment? Increasingly these days, talk of relationship to the natural environment is something one does at free times, on vacations and long weekends. As Jeremy Rifkin (1987, p. 27) points out, "Until the modern era, every concept of time acknowledged an intimate relationship between the rhythms of social life and the rhythms of the earth's ecosystems. . . . While our biological life remains set to the unchanging rhythms of the natural world, our social life has become more and more acclimated to the nanosecond time frame of the computer." Do you believe, as Rifkin does, that human beings have a built-in genetic relationship to the natural world, or do you believe that those are old-fashioned ideas and that with the vast technological development of the present era, human beings can transcend their once vital relationship to the natural world?

What about relationships to the larger society? Does every human being have a natural relationship to the larger society, to some societal entity beyond his or her immediate set of relationships with spouse or partner? If such a relationship to a larger society ought to exist, in what ways do these relationships influence people as learners? How do people begin to resolve concerns of self-interest with concerns of societal interest?

As teachers of adults, what is our position on the developmental literature for adults? Do we accept a certain amount of genetic determinism, which is a part of most developmental theories? For instance, do we accept that during a certain age human beings can expect to do certain things, have particular kinds of thoughts, face certain kinds of dilemmas?

What are our beliefs about how each learner's personal history influences what and how that person will learn? How does a learner's personal history influence the perceptions he or she has about what we are teaching?

To what extent do we believe the social context a learner is in—family, community, work setting—influences what and how the person learns?

Let us go back to Jane and Steve for a moment. What metaphors describe how each of them teaches the article-writing course? Perhaps it is a bit too harsh to do so, but I would suggest that Jane is following the learner-as-machine metaphor. She has in mind specific outcomes from her teaching, and she has well-planned inputs to assist students in achieving the performance outcomes she has identified. Steve's metaphor for adult learners could be described as the traveler on the road of life. The learner essentially knows where he or she is going but needs some help along the way that removes obstacles and perhaps suggests alternatives when crossroads are reached or the path is blurred.

What metaphors do you use to describe the adult learner? A receptacle to be filled with knowledge? A beautiful flower that is watered and cultivated to allow it to express its natural self? A machine? A traveler?

Beliefs About Aims. What ought we to be accomplishing as a teacher of adults? The stock answer often expressed in adult education is that teachers of adults aim to meet adult learner needs. The statement has become a slogan. What does it mean to "meet needs"? Which needs? Human beings have economic, social, biological, political, and spiritual needs. Is it the proper role of the teacher of adults to believe that he or she can meet all these needs? And if not all, which?

We also hear that a proper aim of adult education is to help people learn how to learn. The literature in this area is on the increase, particularly since the work of Robert Smith (1982) helped us to see more clearly what this concept was all about. But, to what extent is helping people learn how to learn a sufficient aim? Are there not situations where it may be equally important to help people learn what to learn as well as how to learn? What about helping people learn why they should learn something? Is this not also a potentially important aim for a teacher of adults? And, finally, are there not also times when we must assist people to unlearn—to rid themselves of old ideas, attitudes, and ways of thinking that prevent certain new learning from occurring?

Another set of fundamental questions about aims relates to learning that is solely for the benefit of the individual and learning that clearly focuses on a societal benefit. Little of the literature on adult education in the United States these days focuses on societal changes as a direct result of educational effort. Paulo Freire's (1970) work is one clear exception. David Boud (1987, p. 226) writes about critical pedagogy and social action: "In this view learning is embedded in a historical, social, and material context. Learners must seek to understand this and transcend the constraints it places on them in order to create an understanding which liberates both themselves and their fellow learners. Learning can never be value-free: it must either work toward supporting the status quo or undermining it and replacing it with something which represents a better form of society." Where do you stand on this issue? The argument often presented for focusing on individual growth and development is this: as individuals learn and grow, they will influence and change society through their individual efforts. But others argue that societal changes occur only when they are consciously focused on. The women's movement and the civil rights movement are often used as examples to make this point. This brings us to another question. To what extent do you believe it is important for you as a teacher of adults to become involved in what often results in controversial issues? To what extent is this an appropriate aim for adult education?

At another level, we sometimes hear teachers of adults saying that their primary aim as a teacher is to transmit information. That is, they as teachers accumulate knowledge, and their role as teachers is to provide it to learners. This is a long-standing view of all teaching. The metaphor often used to describe this teacher role is information delivery system. The teacher serves as a conduit or as a kind of human machine that gathers, stores, and then parcels out bits of information to eager learners. Maxine Greene (1978, p. 38) comments on this aim of teaching: "If [teachers] undergo a purely technical training or a simplified 'competency based' approach, they are likely to see themselves as mere transmission belts—or clerks."

Of course, the information transmission view of teaching often leads to "more efficient" teaching approaches. In contrast to information transmission as purpose, another view is that adult education should empower learners. One approach to empowerment is helping people learn how to learn, as mentioned earlier. Another dimension of empowerment is for learners to experience a transformative experience, as Habermas (1972) and Mezirow (1981) have discussed. There are many more issues that I could raise about aims for adult education, but these examples should suffice to start you thinking about your beliefs in this area. Let us move on to an examination of subject matter.

Beliefs About Subject Matter. At first glance, this area would appear to be of no concern. We are given a teaching assignment—to teach within our area of competency—and we do it. What room is there for issues and alternative perspectives? I suspect that few teachers of adults view subject matter that simplistically. Let me suggest a few of the issues with a brief discussion of each.

At a fundamental level, the subject matter that we teach is a human invention. People have taken their observations of occurrences, their perceptions of events, their thoughts about situations and written about them. The accumulation of these materials becomes subject matter. But, as Loren Eiseley (1970, p. 31) points out, "by naming something, we are creating a prison, a box, a category that prevents us from seeing again more creatively. Often times we are wont to look for categories too soon, to dispense labels prematurely." Eiseley is saying that many of us are quick to develop categories and label them—and that these categories and the labels for them become our subject matter. We as teachers generally dispense this subject matter, seldom questioning, or helping our students to question, the validity of the categories or the accuracy of the labels used to describe events, occurrences, thoughts, and so on.

Another issue that faces many teachers of adults is the extent to which the knowledge that learners have within themselves as a result of their life experiences is valid knowledge for a given learning situation. Some of you are no doubt chuckling because you have long ago accepted learner knowledge as legitimate and important subject matter in your teaching. But there are still those who believe that subject matter is outside the learner and that the role of the teacher is to bring the subject matter to the learning situation. Of course, many of us have resolved this issue by combining the subject matter held by the learners in our groups with the subject matter that we bring as an outsider.

Another way of thinking about this issue is to consider the role of the specialist or expert insofar as subject matter is concerned. On the one hand, some believe that the only subject matter that is legitimate is that expressed by some expert. On the other hand, a body of literature (Compton, 1989) is developing that recognizes the place for and the value of what is called *indigenous knowledge*—the knowledge that is held by nonexperts, people who have accumulated the knowledge through their work and life experience.

An important aside to questions about subject matter is the development of new information storage and retrieval approaches, such as CD-ROM and other optical scan technology, and the relatively recent development of internationally oriented computer data base systems. Almost any person these days has access to tremendous amounts of information on almost any subject imaginable. This information is relatively easily accessible, but it does require a certain amount of technology—and technology costs money. Thus, we see developing issues about not only the role of electronically stored and retrieved information for the teacher of adults but issues of access. What about those persons who cannot afford to use the new technology? And perhaps an even greater issue is what about those adults who do not possess sufficient literacy to use these new information storage systems?

What do you, as a teacher of adults, believe about subject matter in your teaching? What is your position on the issues just raised?

Lastly, my framework is concerned abut teachers and the teaching-learning transaction for adults.

Beliefs About Teachers and the Teaching-Learning Transaction. Here is where we can have fun with metaphors. What metaphor do you use to describe yourself as teacher? Let me give you some examples of metaphors that others have used. For instance, Postman and Weingartner (1969) say that teachers are lamplighters—they attempt to illuminate the minds of their students; gardeners—their goal is to cultivate the mind, nourishing, enhancing the climate, removing barriers, and hoping for growth; muscle builders—exercising and strengthening flabby minds so they can handle the difficult, heavyweight learning tasks they may face in the future; and bucket fillers—pouring information into empty heads and hoping always that the buckets do not leak.

Other common metaphors for the teacher in adult education include travel guide—assisting learners along the path to learning (this metaphor complements the metaphor of the learner as traveler mentioned earlier)—

and factory supervisor—the teacher's metaphor that corresponds to the learner's metaphor of machine-like. The factory supervisor provides sufficient input (instruction provides information) to assure adequate outputs (learning, generally viewed as behavioral change). The factory supervisor is also interested in an efficient operation; that is, the teaching-learning transaction is treated in a businesslike way with most attention given to the bottom line or the outcomes of the learning activity.

Other writers propose other metaphors for the teacher. Tom (1984) talks about the teacher as craftsman, artist, and applied scientist. The craftsman metaphor assumes that the teacher applies mechanical skills to the teaching process, that he or she is able to analyze teaching situations, and that he or she can apply this analytic information to succeeding teaching events. As Tom (1984, p. 101) says, "The ability to analyze teaching situations and the possession of a broad repertoire of teaching strategies seems to distinguish the craftsman teacher from the novice."

The teacher as artist assumes an esthetic dimension to the teaching-learning transaction (Eisner, 1985). Also, the teacher as artist assumes there are no prescriptions for teaching, that the ends for the teaching activity may not be clear at the beginning, and that a certain amount of skill plus creativity is essential for good teaching to occur.

The teacher-as-applied-scientist metaphor assumes that the educator will think of teaching as applying research findings to problems of teaching. Unfortunately, research findings on teaching are often inconclusive and even contradictory. Besides, research in teaching often focuses on one or two variables, and thus it is often difficult to apply the findings in broader, more complicated practical teaching situations. Nevertheless, this metaphor for teaching has gotten considerable attention in adult education in the hope that one day many of the teaching problems in adult education can be answered by research findings. Others, myself included, are not so sure that scientific research can ever answer even a majority of teaching problems.

Which of these metaphors for the teacher comes closest to what you believe? Or is there another metaphor that better describes how you see yourself as teacher?

Examining what we believe about the teaching-learning transaction is a natural outgrowth of examining what we believe about the role of teacher. Indeed, there is an obvious overlap. What we believe about our role as teacher is generally directly related to what we believe about teaching adults and about adult learning.

One approach to analyzing what we believe about the teaching and learning transaction is to examine our own preferred approach to learning. Some of us prefer a more intuitive approach to learning—looking first at the whole before examining the pieces. Others prefer a more rational approach—beginning with the pieces and then putting them together to form the whole. Some people prefer to learn in groups; others believe they learn better by themselves. Some prefer hearing a lecturer as the best way of learning. Others prefer "seeing," as by watching a videotape or a film. Still others prefer hands-on direct manipulation of materials for most beneficial learning. We could go on.

I believe that it is important for the teachers of adults to reflect on their own preferred learning approach. Many of us believe that how we learn best is how others learn best. However, research evidence on learning style suggests there is a considerable range of learning style preferences and that people do not all learn in the same way.

Although I said that I would not deal with definitions, I make an exception here. You may very well want to wrestle with your definition of adult learning, because your definition is likely to be the beacon that guides your teaching. Some common definitions include: accumulation of information; change in behavior; improved performance; change in knowledge, attitudes, and skill; a new sense of meaning; personal transformation; and cognitive restructuring. Whichever of these definitions or whatever combination of these definitions we hold most certainly influences how we teach. My point is not to suggest that any of these definitions is right or wrong but to encourage you as teacher to identify your own definition and then examine it to see if this is what you really believe adult learning is all about.

Of course, the real-life situation is more complicated than simply one of identifying, evaluating, and then following your definition of adult learning with appropriate teaching approaches. The institution, agency, or firm in which you work has its own definition of adult learning; implicitly or explicitly, it has in mind what adults ought be gaining from your teaching. If you work as a trainer in a business and have responsibility for teaching employees new skills, then skill development is what is expected. Your own personal definition of adult learning may come into conflict with your employer's definition. In my experience, this happens often. But, until you have examined your own foundations about teaching and learning, you may have a nagging feeling that something is wrong without being able to say what it is. An analysis of your own beliefs about teaching and learning can bring the source of your unease to the surface.

Working Philosophy

Identifying and examining what you believe as a teacher of adults can have many benefits. Such an analysis can lead to the development of your working philosophy of adult education, a solid foundation to undergird your everyday practice. A working philosophy is, of course, more than merely working out what you believe about learners, aims, subject matter, and the teaching-learning transaction. There is a strong relationship among the various elements of the framework. What you believe about adults as learners, their potential, and their reasons for learning will influence how you view the teaching-learning process. What you see as the role for subject matter is likely to influence what you believe is the aim for what you do, and so on.

Your working philosophy may change—indeed, in most instances it will change—as you face new challenges and problems. But the process for examining and fine-tuning your beliefs can serve as a constant.

References

Apps, J. *Toward A Working Philosophy of Adult Education.* Syracuse, New York: Syracuse University Publications in Continuing Education, 1973.

Apps, J. *Problems in Continuing Education.* New York: McGraw-Hill, 1979.

Apps, J. *Improving Practice in Continuing Education: Modern Approaches for Understanding the Field and Determining Priorities.* San Francisco: Jossey-Bass, 1985.

Apps, J. *Higher Education in a Learning Society: Meeting New Demands for Education and Training.* San Francisco: Jossey-Bass, 1988.

Bem, D. *Beliefs, Attitudes, and Human Affairs.* Belmont, Calif.: Brooks/Cole, 1970.

Berry, W. *The Unsettling of America: Culture and Agriculture.* New York: Avon Books, 1977.

Boud, D. "A Facilitator's View of Adult Learning." In D. Boud and V. Griffen (eds.), *Appreciating Adults Learning.* London: Kogan Page, 1987.

Compton, J. L. (ed.). *The Transformation of International Agricultural Research and Development.* Boulder, Colo.: Lynne Rienner, 1989.

Eiseley, L. *The Invisible Pyramid.* New York: Scribner's, 1970.

Eisner, E. W. *The Educational Imagination.* (2nd ed.) New York: Macmillan, 1985.

Freire, P. *Pedagogy of the Oppressed.* New York: Herder and Herder, 1970.

Greene, M. *Landscapes of Learning.* New York: Teachers College Press, 1978.

Habermas, J. *Knowledge and Human Interests.* Boston: Beacon Press, 1972.

Mezirow, J. D. "A Critical Theory of Adult Learning and Education." *Adult Education,* 1981, *32* (1), 3–24.

Postman, N., and Weingartner, C. *Teaching as a Subversive Activity.* New York: Dell, 1969.

Rifkin, J. *Time Wars.* New York: Henry Holt, 1987.

Scheffler, I. *The Language of Education.* Springfield, Ill.: C. C. Thomas, 1960.

Smith, R. *Learning How to Learn.* Chicago: Follett, 1982.

Tom, A. R. *Teaching as a Moral Craft.* New York: Longman, 1984.

Jerold W. Apps is professor of adult and continuing education at the University of Wisconsin, Madison, and the author of several books on adult education.

Using teaching style information and learning style information together requires consideration of multiple concerns.

Using Learning Style Information, Too

L. Adrianne Bonham

The idea of doing something with teaching styles is popular today among adult educators. So is the idea of doing something with learning styles. I say *doing something with* because the ideas of what to do are so diverse that there is no more specific phrase that seems to include all the possibilities.

Would it not be convenient, for instance, that a program planner could improve learning just by assessing learner A's learning style and assigning her to a teacher who uses a corresponding teaching style? Or, perhaps teacher B, who is already assigned to teach learner A, could be persuaded to change his teaching style in order to achieve the match.

The trouble is that neither research nor everyday experience supports those strategies as ways to increase learning. There are not even theories that suggest that it is simple to determine how to match teacher to learner on the basis of style. Let us first consider some of the ideas about what learning styles are, how they affect learning, and how they should be taken into account.

Learning Styles

While educators generally agree that learning style is the characteristic way in which a learner operates within the learning situation, there

E. R. Hayes (ed.). *Effective Teaching Styles.*
New Directions for Continuing Education, no. 43. San Francisco: Jossey-Bass, Fall 1989.

are many ideas about what the styles are and how style information should be used. One point of confusion concerns the terms *cognitive style* and *learning style*. In this chapter, I use the term *learning style* to refer to both.

To give an idea of the variety of these ideas, a few of the theories used by adult educators are identified in Table 1. One helpful scheme for organizing individual theories into a pattern is given by Claxton and Murrell (1987). The categories in their scheme are designed to reflect the distance of theories from the core of personality and thus the amount of flexibility or deliberate change that might be possible.

Many learning style theorists emphasize that people learn more and enjoy their classroom experiences more when they can use their preferred learning styles. Sometimes emphasis is placed on the penalty paid by learners when classroom activities are incompatible with their characteristic ways of learning. As will be shown, there are some reasons to question these judgments, and there are other possible interpretations.

A popular idea for the use of style information is to identify the styles of learners and then choose teaching methods that match the various styles. Another idea is to educate learners about their own styles and help them expand the range of styles with which they feel comfortable. This chapter explores these options and some others.

Concerns Prior to Application

Before deciding on how to combine teaching style and learning style theories in the classroom, a teacher should explore five questions: What are we matching? What is the purpose of the learning? What effect does the learning content have? What other individual differences enter the equation? What is the evidence that matching works?

What Are We Matching? There may be a question about the comparability of a given learning style instrument (or theory) and a given teaching style instrument (or theory). In some cases, the same instrument is used to describe the teacher and the learner. For instance, the Embedded Figures Test (EFT) can determine that a teacher is field independent and that some learners are, too (Witkin, Moore, Goodenough, and Cox, 1977). In other instances, there are companion instruments. For example, the Canfield Instructional Styles Inventory (Canfield and Canfield, 1976a) measures the teacher's preference on seventeen dimensions, and the Canfield Learning Styles Inventory (Canfield and Canfield, 1976b) measures the learners' preferences on seventeen dimensions. Most of the dimensions are the same.

Using the same instrument for teacher and learner makes it clear what is being matched. If they are good, instruments that measure the

Table 1. Learning Style Theories and Instruments

Theory	Psychological differentiation	Educational cognitive style	(Related to) experiential learning	Personality types (Jung)	(Related to college classroom learning)	(Related to children's classroom learning)	?
Instrument	Embedded Figures Test, Group Embedded Figures Test	Cognitive Style Interest Inventory	Learning Style Inventory	Myers-Briggs Type Indicator	Grasha-Riechmann Student Learning Styles Scale	Productivity Environmental Preference Survey	Learning Styles Inventory
Style elements	Field independent, field dependent	Symbols and their meanings (22 elements), cultural determinants (3), modalities of inference (5)	Accommodator, diverger, assimilator, converger	Extravert/introvert, sensing/intuitive, thinking/feeling, perceiving/judging	Independent/ dependent, collaborative/ competitive, participant/ avoidant	Immediate environment (4 elements), emotionality (4), sociological needs (4), physical needs (9)	Conditions (4 elements, each with 2 choices), content (4 elements), mode (4), expectation
Item type	Geometric shapes to be matched	Likert-type scale	Rank alternatives	Forced choice	Likert-type scale	Likert-type scale	Rank alternatives
Subjects for norming	Wide variety adults and children	College students	Business managers, occupational groups, grad/ undergrad students	Wide variety adults and children	Unknown; assume college students	Adults (not otherwise described)	Not stated
Reference	Witkin, Moore, Goodenough, and Cox, 1977	Nunney, 1978	Kolb, 1976	Myers and McCaulley, 1985	Grasha, 1972	Price, Dunn, and Dunn, 1982	Canfield, 1983

same dimensions with separate instruments for teacher and learner also make it clear. However, problems can exist when one set of dimensions for the teacher must be correlated with a different set for the learner. Given the individuality of theorists, there is seldom a close match between independently developed theories, even when styles carry the same label. Thus, it would be at least risky to use the EFT to measure a teacher's field independence and the Grasha-Riechmann Student Learning Styles Scales (GRSLSS) (Family Resource Center, 1975) to measure a learner's independence. These two instruments illustrate one problem in particular. As Claxton and Murrell (1987) have shown, field independence is near the core of the personality and thus difficult to alter, while the GRSLSS's independence must be on the outer fringes, because it can be changed by one semester's experience in one class (Grasha, 1972).

One other option for matching already has been mentioned: measure the learner's learning style, and match it with a teaching method. For instance, the person who prefers to learn by listening may be assigned to a teacher who consistently uses the lecture method. The chief problem with this kind of matching seems to be difficulty in determining which combinations of style and method are matches and which are mismatches. Consider, for instance, an experiment that shows no difference in amount of learning from lecture for persons who prefer auditory learning and for persons who prefer visual learning. The problem may be that the person with a preference for visual learning learned as much as the person with a preference for auditory learning because the teacher used overhead cells and wrote on the chalkboard or because the learner studied notes taken during the lecture. Researchers have pointed out that most learners, most of the time, alter a teaching method for themselves so that it comes closer to fitting their preferences or strengths.

What Is the Purpose of the Learning? If there is an overriding need for someone to learn specific content quickly—for instance, for a person to learn how to operate a new piece of equipment—planners should do everything possible to help the person accomplish that immediate goal. Matching would be especially appropriate if the person had failed in an earlier attempt to learn the same skill. There would be ample justification for sticking with the learner's preferred learning style and for making all possible adjustments to the teacher's teaching style.

In many cases, however, there is an equal or greater need for the learner to become a more resourceful learner. Then, the learner may be better served by practicing less comfortable styles and by learning to accommodate other influences, such as the style of the teacher or the style that best fits certain content. In other words, it is simplistic to say that matching learner style with teacher style is always the best approach.

In adult education, perhaps in all education, there is more than one relevant definition of success in the learning situation. The purpose discussed in the last two paragraphs is increased learning. Another desired outcome, which is especially relevant in the kind of continuing education that is not mandatory for the learner, is learner satisfaction. Unfortunately, research has shown that what is best for increasing learning may not be what is best for increasing satisfaction (Long, 1985). Matching learners' styles may produce more comfortable (satisfying) learning, but certain mismatches may challenge the learner to more effective performance. In fact, interpreters of the Myers-Briggs Type Indicator (MBTI) make precisely this point about persons working in task-related groups (Myers and McCaulley, 1985). Those who have the same profiles on the MBTI are said to enjoy working together but to learn less effectively because they reinforce one another's weaknesses. Persons with some differences challenge one another's weaknesses, and, while they may be somewhat uncomfortable, they actually have the potential to learn more.

What Effect Does the Learning Content Have? A certain kind of content may call for one learning style over another. For instance, a sequential approach may be important in math learning, while a holistic approach may produce greater learning in a painting class. While this question bears on decisions about what approach to take in individual learning situations, it also points up the need for learners to develop style flexibility. There will be times when the learner is penalized if he or she is unable to adopt the style that is demanded by the content.

What Other Individual Differences Enter the Equation? There are individual differences beyond those usually labeled learning style. They should be considered when the teacher decides how to take style into account. For instance, a person with marginal mental abilities may need to have more adjustments made for his or her style than a person with more mental resources.

Without regard to ability, some learners and some teachers are less flexible in their use of preferred styles. They are so entrenched in a style that using a different one would cause major blocks in their teaching or learning approaches. While the long-range goal should be increased flexibility, a realistic view of a given learning situation may have to take this lack of flexibility into account. In fact, it may be that degree of flexibility will some day be defined as an aspect of teaching and learning styles.

A slightly different issue is one of strength of preference. Some theorists say that only the strongly held preferences must be taken into account, even if style matching is the advocated approach (Price, Dunn, and Dunn, 1982). Most instruments produce continuous scores that indicate strength of preference as well as preferred style. The farther a score is from the midpoint, the stronger is the preference. If some learners score near the midpoint on an instrument, it may be that the teacher will find it unnecessary and unproductive to go to the trouble of adjusting teaching style for these persons.

What Is the Evidence That Matching Works? A great variety of outcomes has resulted from experimental efforts to match learning styles with some pattern of teacher behavior, whether that pattern is described as style or as teaching method. One reason for such variety may be that researchers have made different assumptions about the four questions just discussed.

While research matching style to style is somewhat scarce, there is more research that deals with the matching of learning style to specific teaching methods. This body of research is usually identified with the term *aptitude-treatment interaction*. In terms of structuring the research, the styles are aptitudes, and the teaching methods are treatments (Cronbach and Snow, 1977; Messick and Associates, 1984). The usual hypothesis is that one method produces better results for persons with a style that "matches" the method, while another method produces better results for another style. Unfortunately, as the literature reviews show (Cronbach and Snow, 1977; Doyle and Rutherford, 1984), the results have been inconsistent. It is frequently found that persons with one style outperform others, regardless of which teaching method is used. For instance, Charlton (1980), who used the MBTI as the measure of style, expected that sensing students would benefit more from structured learning activities than intuitives would but found that intuitives learned better than sensing students regardless of the teaching method used.

Why Style Information Should Be Used

To this point, the chief purpose has been to show that there is no justification for jumping on a style bandwagon, especially one that carries only a single style theory and a single idea about how to use style information. Nevertheless, I believe that there is benefit in taking style—teaching and learning—into account when planning for learning. The strongest reason for doing so, it seems to me, is the possibility of producing a Hawthorne effect. Let me explain.

Some years ago, researchers were trying to determine the optimum conditions needed for a manufacturing program at the Hawthorne plant of Western Electric Company. In an experimental sequence that they considered to be tightly controlled, they varied the working conditions from week to week. To their consternation, every change was followed by increased productivity. They finally decided that the cause of the increases, which came to be known as the *Hawthorne effect*, was that employees worked harder because they knew they were the subjects of some sort of research related to productivity (Ary, Jacobs, and Razavieh, 1979; Wolman, 1973). I must question why the researchers considered their experiment a failure. After all, they succeeded in increasing productivity.

I believe the best reason currently available for using style information is its potential Hawthorne effect. In reading anecdotal reports about the benefits of using style information, I am often struck by how much energy and creativity the teachers and learners put into planning and conducting the learning. They were excited about something new and promising. They liked to learn more about themselves and about how they taught or learned. As a result, the "treatment" was said to enhance learning and satisfaction.

It is irrelevant that the label of *treatment* is most often given to the matching approach. Whatever is labeled *treatment* may prove effective if one assumes that the treatment is the only way in which situations differ. What actually enhances learning is that teachers and learners give careful and enthusiastic attention to the learning process instead of continuing to take the process for granted and giving all their attention to the content to be learned.

How Style Information Can Be Used

Keeping in mind that the overall purpose is to stimulate teachers' and learners' interest in the learning process, here are some ideas to consider in relation to teaching and learning styles.

Choose Instruments Deliberately. Style instruments do not have a good reputation for reliability and validity. Furthermore, some do not have a strong theoretical framework (Bonham, 1987). Before choosing instruments, try to determine what work has gone into developing them, what criticisms have been published, and with whom they are intended to be used. You will also have to be concerned about such logistical considerations as how long it takes to administer, score, and interpret the instruments.

Furthermore, choose instruments to measure teaching and learning styles that seem most relevant to your teaching situation. Relevance is affected by such considerations as the content to be taught, the educational level and other characteristics of learners and teachers, and the options for change within the situation. For instance, there is no use asking if learners prefer to eat or drink while learning, as the Productivity Environmental Preference Survey does, if there is an inviolable rule against having food and drink in the classroom. Kolb's Learning Style Inventory, like a number of other inventories, was developed for use with college students. A teacher should be cautious about using it with learners who have limited experience in formal education. The Canfield LSI contains a large portion of items dealing with expectations about grades. These seem irrelevant to persons in a class being taken for enjoyment.

If you plan to use both a teaching style instrument and a learning style instrument, be sure they go together. For instance, several learning style instruments GRSLSS, EFT, PEPS, Canfield LSI have a dimension similar to independence/dependence, but there is little evidence that they measure the same characteristic and that they can be used interchangeably.

Develop Interpretation Skills. Having chosen one or several instruments, spend time learning to interpret the underlying theories. Give special attention to how the styles interact with content or with the particular characteristics of the kinds of learners whom you expect to teach.

Let me illustrate from my own experience. In teaching undergraduate journalism classes, I administered a measure of Jungian types. I was then able to explain to some students why they wanted to write "think" pieces and why their editor had to push them to go out and interview people: they were introverts. In contrast, the extroverts liked doing the interviews. They hated sitting alone to write the stories and often came to the deadline with only their original notes. Such interpretations seemed to help students understand themselves and others, use their strengths, work on their weaknesses, and be tolerant of the styles of other students.

Perhaps one reason why research has not supported the benefits of considering style is that insufficient credit has been given to the role of the teacher as a style expert. However, I have a certain kind of expert in mind. I react with trepidation toward the enthusiastic advocate of a single instrument and prescription. Too often, that person has accepted the word of the instrument's salesperson and has no awareness of the broad field of research and theory building. I feel safer with an expert who states caveats, who knows about and uses more than one theory, and who spends considerable energy determining how certain theories relate to the particular subject matter in question. This is the person who can use style information at relevant points throughout the learning process without having to convince learners that style is the only relevant issue in learning.

Discuss the Scores and What They Mean. I believe that the most important component in the process of using style information is discussing it with learners. This usually means taking class time to administer the instrument and to interpret the theory to learners. It also means that the teacher shares information about his or her own style and explores with learners the possible uses of style information in planning and conducting the learning (Davidman, 1984). Furthermore, you can plan in advance ways that you will use the information; and you can give chances for learners to use self-management skills (Friedman and Alley, 1984; Messick, 1985).

Again, let me share my own experience. In a graduate class in adult education, I administered the Kolb Learning Style Inventory, interpreted it to students, and assigned students to work groups on the basis of their learning styles. I explained that, while matching styles might make learners more comfortable, forming groups to include contrasting styles might help to improve learning. If all members tended to be more reflective than active, the group might spend too much time trying to define and refine its purpose. If all members had the opposite inclinations, they might busily set about their work without having defined it clearly. A mixture of styles should produce a profitable dialectic. During the course, time was given to reflect on how learning style might be affecting the product or the satisfaction of group members while recognizing that style was only one factor at work in such a situation.

Plan for Skill Development. A largely overlooked component of style use is the need to learn certain skills in order to adopt some styles. Such style as field independence is an ability, because it is measured by whether and how rapidly the learner is able to find simple geometric figures within complex ones. Such a style as auditory preference requires some ability: the ability to process mentally information that is only heard.

In adult education, we rightly deemphasize the need for complex skills or certain levels of intelligence, because many adults are threatened either by memories of their perceived lack of ability in school or by fears that their abilities are declining with age. To get around those stereotyped reactions, we can use the concept of style—a certain way of learning rather than a certain amount of ability to learn. Nevertheless, there are many teaching and learning styles that require skills, and those skills can be learned.

You can help learners broaden their effective range of styles by planning activities that allow them to practice needed skills in relation to the content that you teach. For instance, I have asked intuitive journalism students to write personality sketches by describing only what they saw. The aim was to help them overcome their habit of reporting their intuitive perceptions; they had to develop consciously the skill of reporting specific pieces of information that would cause the reader to reach the same perceptions that they had reached intuitively.

Perhaps one reason teachers hold onto the lecture method and other styles that keep them in control is that they have not developed the skills needed to carry on a meaningful discussion with learners. Those skills, which all can be practiced, include understanding what another person is saying, thinking quickly of ways to direct discussion toward certain points, and knowing how to keep individuals from dominating the discussion.

Adapt for Short Formats. You may wonder how to deal with style when you see learners only for a few hours, a weekend, or a week. One way is to administer and score the style instrument before the event for preregistered participants. You can even provide written style interpretation in advance if the instrument is self-scoring. Another approach is not to use an instrument but to provide the kind of oral interpretation of a theory, such as Kolb's, that leads learners to examine and label their own styles.

If you are able to measure styles at one time but not at another, you may develop profiles of typical participants. These can be the basis for your interpretation to new groups of learners and for your planning of methods and approaches. Even if you cannot spend conference time measuring or interpreting styles, you can build style information into your presentation so that learners think about their own learning processes.

Do Some Research. I do not know of research that supports the suggestions I have offered here. A few studies have dealt with the effect of revealing style information to learners, and the results did not show that the effort was profitable (Fourier, 1983, 1984). However, in those situations the person doing the revealing was not the teacher of a class in which learning or satisfaction was to be measured.

There are other reasons why it might not be easy to show effects in a quantitative study. Multiple factors may interact with styles. For instance, certain combinations of teaching and learning styles may produce one effect in learners with above-average intelligence and another effect in learners with below-average intelligence (Entwistle, 1981; Tomlinson, 1985). While such factors as ability can be held constant when they are known, identification of several potentially influential factors complicates the study by multiplying the number of subjects needed.

One measure of a good experimental study is that the various groups are alike except for the treatment. However, any attempt to limit the treatment to something like an hour of style interpretation at the beginning of the class would not be what I have in mind as a meaningful application of style information. A teacher trying to enhance the Hawthorne effect would be prepared to change any number of features of the learning experience because of what was revealed about teacher and learner styles. It may not be possible to capture the subtle differences between teaching situations through a rationalistic research design that focuses attention on a few variables (Tomlinson, 1985).

Another limitation of most rationalistic research is that results must be measured within a short time after the treatment is applied. However, it is possible that the Hawthorne effect increases over time as the learner confronts learning situations that cause further thought about styles. Furthermore, the teacher may gain skill in interpreting style information so that later "treatments" are more effective than earlier ones.

Perhaps qualitative methods, such as case studies, would be more effective than quantitative research methods. The question of what is happening may be more relevant than the question of whether a specific outcome is being achieved.

Action research is also needed. In such research, the concern is with solving a problem, not with testing a research question or hypothesis. Thus, the researcher is free to adapt the "treatment" as the research progresses. Results can be tested by a variety of methods throughout the research, and they become guidance for further interventions (Merriam and Simpson, 1984).

You can try out various style instruments, hone your skills at interpreting and incorporating style information, and test the effectiveness of certain style-flexing or skill-building activities. Such research may not be generalizable to other settings, as action research often is not. However, it can be useful to you as you develop skills to enhance your teaching.

Summary

Important and troubling issues in style theory and research make it unwise to use the approach of matching teaching style (*or* teaching method) to learners' styles unquestioningly. However, there are other ways to use style information.

A potentially valuable approach is to make learners and teachers aware of style in order to focus attention and creativity on the learning process. Practitioners can use a variety of instruments that seem relevant to the teachers, learners, content, and context involved in specific continuing education situations. Keys to success are the expertise developed by the teacher and the sense of exploration and excitement brought to the learning environment by a positive emphasis on individual differences.

References

Ary, D., Jacobs, L. C., and Razavieh, A. *Introduction to Research in Education.* (2nd ed.). New York: Holt, Rinehart and Winston, 1979.

Bonham, L. A. "Theoretical and Practical Differences and Similarities Among Selected Cognitive and Learning Styles of Adults: An Analysis of the Literature." *Dissertation Abstracts International*, 1987, *48*, 2788A.

Canfield, A. A. *Canfield Learning Styles Inventory, Form S-A Manual.* Birmingham, Mich.: Humanics Media, 1983.

Canfield, A. A., and Canfield, J. S. *Instructional Styles Inventory.* Ann Arbor, Mich.: Humanics Media, 1976a.

Canfield, A. A., and Canfield, J. S. *Learning Styles Inventory.* Ann Arbor, Mich.: Humanics Media, 1976b.

Charlton, R. E. "Cognitive Style Considerations for the Improvement of Biology Education." *American Biology Teacher*, 1980, *42*, 244–247.

Claxton, C. S., and Murrell, P. H. *Learning Styles: Implications for Improving Educational Practices.* ASHE-ERIC Higher Education Report No. 4. Washington, D.C.: Association for the Study of Higher Education, 1987.

Cronbach, L. J., and Snow, R. E. *Aptitudes and Instructional Methods: A Handbook for Research on Interactions.* New York: Irvington, 1977.

Davidman, L. *Learning Style and Teaching Style Analysis in the Teacher Education Curriculum: A Synthesis Approach.* San Luis Obispo: Education Department, California Polytechnic State University, 1984. (ED 249 183)

Doyle, W., and Rutherford, B. "Classroom Research on Matching Learning and Teaching Styles." *Theory into Practice*, 1984, *23*, 20–25.

Entwistle, N. *Styles of Learning and Teaching: An Integrative Outline of Educational Psychology for Students, Teachers, and Lecturers.* New York: Wiley, 1981.

Family Resource Center. *Grasha-Riechmann Student Learning Style Questionnaire: Specific Class Form*. Cincinnati: Family Resource Center, University of Cincinnati, 1975.

Fourier, M. J. "Academic Achievement of Students Who Receive Disclosure of Cognitive Style Map Information." *Journal of Experimental Education*, 1983, *51*, 122–130.

Fourier, M. J. "Disclosure of Cognitive Style Information: Effects on Achievement of Adult Learners." *Adult Education Quarterly*, 1984, *34*, 147–154.

Friedman, P., and Alley, R. "Learning/Teaching Styles: Applying the Principles." *Theory into Practice*, 1984, *23*, 77–81.

Grasha, A. F. "Observations on Relating Teaching Goals to Student Response Styles and Classroom Methods. *American Psychologist*, 1972, *27*, 144–147.

Kolb, D. A. *Learning Style Inventory Technical Manual*. Boston: McBer, 1976.

Long, H. B. "Contradictory Expectations? Achievement and Satisfaction in Adult Learning." *Journal of Continuing Higher Education*, 1985, *33* (3), 10–12.

Merriam, S. B., and Simpson, E. L. *A Guide to Research for Educators and Trainers of Adults*. Malabar, Fla.: Krieger, 1984.

Messick, S. "Style in the Interplay of Structure and Process." In N. Entwistle (ed.), *New Directions in Educational Psychology 1: Learning and Teaching*. London: Falmer Press, 1985.

Messick, S., and Associates. *Individuality in Learning*. Ann Arbor, Mich.: Books on Demand UMI, n.d.

Myers, I. B., and McCaulley, M. H. *Manual: A Guide to the Development and Use of the Myers-Briggs Type Indicator*. Palo Alto, Calif.: Consulting Psychologists Press, 1985.

Nunney, D. N. "Cognitive Style Mapping." *Training and Development Journal*, 1978, *32* (9), 50–57.

Price, G. E., Dunn, R. S., and Dunn, K. J. *Productivity Environmental Preference Survey Manual*. Lawrence, Kans.: Price Systems, 1982.

Tomlinson, P. "Matching Learning and Teaching: The Interactive Approach in Educational Psychology." In N. Entwistle (ed.), *New Directions in Educational Psychology 1: Learning and Teaching*. London: Falmer Press, 1985.

Witkin, H. A., Moore, C.A.K., Goodenough, D. R., and Cox, P. W. "Field-Dependent and Field-Independent Cognitive Styles and Their Educational Implications." *Review of Educational Research*, 1977, *47*, 1–64.

Wolman, B. B. (ed.) *Dictionary of Behavioral Science*. New York: Van Nostrand Reinhold, 1973.

L. Adrianne Bonham is assistant professor of adult and extension education at Texas A & M University.

A personally constructed model can help teachers make effective instructional use of information technology without sacrificing important aspects of their teaching styles.

Teaching Styles and Technology

Barbara M. Florini

For over a decade, the tools of communication or information technology have become more widely available, less expensive, and easier to use. Computer, laser disc, video, audio, and telecommunication technologies have opened new ways for generating, processing, storing, and exchanging information whether simple or abstruse. Through these and other information tools, adult educators working in diverse settings can reach previously underserved learners and generally provide students with more dynamic learning experiences. Less clear than these obvious benefits, however, are any potential repercussions on important matters like the teaching-learning process, administration, and curriculum and course design or the effects on students, the effects on teachers, and problems of equitable access for learners.

McCreary and Van Duren (1987) and Harasim (1987) are among the educators addressing some of these concerns. This chapter focuses on possible effects that using technology has on teachers and their preferred teaching styles. Experience suggests that instructors sometimes find it necessary to adjust their teaching styles when using technology, but little is known about any consequences for teachers or learning outcomes. The intent here is to begin an exploration of this topic whose potential significance warrants further attention. Administrators should also find

E. R. Hayes (ed.). *Effective Teaching Styles.*
New Directions for Continuing Education, no. 43. San Francisco: Jossey-Bass, Fall 1989.

the chapter of interest. As more agency heads, program directors, and planners weigh the instructional uses of information technology, they will want to consider all pertinent variables, including possible effects on teachers.

This chapter has three main sections. The first is a brief survey of information technology, the second discusses teaching styles and technology, and the third describes a framework for building a personal model for using technology. Assuming that a teacher's style represents characteristic behavior that is stable over time and across circumstances (see Chapter One of this volume), it is worth inquiring how teaching styles might be affected when different information technologies are introduced into the teaching process. Before pursuing this, however, we need a brief survey of information technology and some of its components.

Information Technology

Information technology encompasses a heterogeneous array of separate technologies that include computer, telecommunication, laser disc, audio, and video technology. Each has some capacity for storing, processing, or disseminating information. Because people are increasingly able to link the individual capabilities of these technologies, information usable by one becomes available to all. Thus, information can be manipulated and distributed in unprecedented ways. The social, political, and economic implications are scarcely comprehended (Brand, 1987; Donnelly, 1986).

In addition to its visible components, information technology has other aspects that can be explored from diverse perspectives. Philosophers inquire into the nature and meaning of information technology. Sociologists are concerned with its social implications. Political theorists contemplate its significance for governance. Some educators use information technology to improve practice in different ways. This section focuses on selected computer and video information tools that adult educators are finding useful for reaching additional learners and for providing all students with enriched learning experiences.

The versatility of video and computer technologies makes them popular choices for use in adult education. Components of the two technologies can be variously configured and even combined, thereby providing educators with many potential applications. Possible video or computer system configurations range from those manageable by an individual to quite complex ones requiring a support team.

For example, video systems span a configuration continuum anchored at one end by items like hand-held cameras and familiar VCRs and at the other by sophisticated studio systems designed for two-way interactive televised programs. Potential applications include both live broadcasts and taped productions, any of which may be intended for both formal and informal learning situations. The live broadcasts may or may not involve two-way communication. The videotapes can be mailed to distant learners or kept in a central location on site for viewing at students' convenience.

Computer systems, too, show a wide range of configurations that extends from limited microcomputers to supercomputers with extraordinary processing powers. Like video, computer technology can be used by itself or combined in various ways with other technologies. For instance, teachers can use a microcomputer in conjunction with compact disc or video laser disc technology to offer students new dimensions of interactive instruction. Through microcomputers or mainframe computers, teachers can provide on-site students with computer-based instruction and, in conjunction with telecommunications, reach distant learners as well. Today an instructor can also combine the use of a microcomputer, a mainframe, and telecommunications to engage widely dispersed students in asynchronous group discussions. That is, participants can read other students' contributions to any of several topics and enter their own comments when convenient. In addition to storing messages in their intended slots, the computer program makes it easy for the instructor to facilitate class discussion. This is called *computer conferencing*, and it will be discussed in more detail later.

The extent to which instructors' preferred teaching styles can be influenced by the use of technology depends upon the specific technology, the conditions of its use, the teacher's understanding of it, and his or her determination to use a preferred teaching style. The following overview of three popular information technologies provides some background for further discussion of this notion. The three technologies examined here are computer-assisted interactive video, computer conferencing, and video-based lessons. These technologies were selected because of their versatility, growing availability, or potential utility for adult educators. Collectively, the three help illustrate the sheer multiplicity of technological options teachers have available in this information age.

Computer-Assisted Interactive Video (CAIV). A technology that combines the power of computers with that of video intuitively appeals to many educators who envision unique, lively, interactive learning possibilities for students. The video component can show dynamic processes, such as people interacting or the flow of weather patterns; worlds like the ocean floor, Amazon jungle, or human body; and masterpieces from a famous art collection. In short, anything that can be captured by a video camera is potentially available for the educators' use. With the computer component, educators can use their professional judgments to organize and manage the instruction as they think best.

Basically, a CAIV system consists of a microcomputer, a videodisc or videotape player, a device that lets the computer control the player, an assortment of cables, a computer program for writing and executing lessons, and a videodisc or videotape with appropriate motion and still visuals. Both videodiscs and videotapes also have sound channels. There are a number of computer programs of varying complexity designed for use by nonprogrammers who wish to develop CAIV lessons. Over the past several years, an assortment of videodiscs intended for educational purposes has appeared on the market. Educators have the additional option of preparing a videotape and having a videodisc made from it— a fairly expensive, time-consuming process.

Instructors may find existing computer-assisted interactive packages satisfactory and available for use. The only decision facing teachers then is how to integrate the technology-based instruction into their teaching process. In other cases, they may identify an educational problem they believe best addressed by using CAIV but for which there are no extant materials. Whether commercially available or locally produced, CAIV instruction is expensive due to associated equipment, material, and human resource costs. Instructors will have to decide if the problem's importance justifies the price.

Instruction based on a combination of microcomputer and videodisc or even videotape can provide students with dynamic multisensory, individualized, and interactive learning activities. Use of CAIV especially adds new dimensions of reality to simulations. Due to the video, students can see and hear an event unfold. Depending upon how the computer is programmed, it could let them respond to the situation and receive feedback on their responses. From these responses, the computer could determine whether to move individual students to a repetition of the event, to a variant presentation of it, or on to a new situation. Alternatively, the computer could be programmed to let learners control how they proceed through the lesson. Many computer programs used for CAIV can also keep records of a student's progress through each lesson.

Computer-assisted interactive video has other distinct characteristics worth noting here. Because of the video production and computer programming involved, CAIV material is not readily edited or updated. The nature of today's videodiscs precludes altering material once in place, and programming is both time-consuming and costly. An instructor selecting extant materials can therefore be constrained by the original producer's instructional design. As indicated earlier, a computer can be programmed to control how students progress through a lesson. Such an authoritarian approach is not compatible with the teaching styles of many adult educators. An instructor who prefers that students have control can only decide whether the material is sufficiently valuable to use anyway. Altering it is not a realistic option. Similarly, an instructor dissatisfied with the nature of the feedback from computer to student can do little to alter it. Some may find creative ways to compensate for these kinds of problems by how they structure other activities, but the burden to do so is on them. Others may elect to create their own lessons, a costly and laborious undertaking that usually requires assistance from support personnel who are experts in video production, CAIV lesson design, and computer programming. Such action does have the clear advantage of having instruction designed for compatibility with a preferred teaching style. But, whether using prepackaged CAIV materials or creating their own, teachers need an awareness of the fixed nature of CAIV lessons.

Additional characteristics have important logistical implications for teachers. CAIV equipment is both costly and bulky. Even with today's cheaper and miniaturized electronics, the combination of microcomputer, video player, monitor, and assorted peripherals is an expensive and scarcely portable package. The equipment may be located in sites that are open only during fixed times. Teachers will have to calculate how much time their classes will need to complete the lessons given the number of students, the number of CAIV stations, the amount of time each student needs to complete the lessons, and the amount of time the equipment is available. In some cases, teachers will have to make special arrangements for students whose schedules prevent them from using the equipment during the regularly scheduled hours.

Through CAIV, teachers can provide uniquely dynamic learning experiences. But, as with other information technologies, there are trade-offs. Professional judgment applied in specific circumstances is needed to weigh the benefits and costs.

Computer Conferencing. Basically, computer conferencing is a form of computer-based telecommunication that facilitates group discussion. Some government departments and businesses have been using computer conferencing for well over a decade to help dispersed personnel conduct work-related discussions (Vallee, 1984). In application, conferencing combines the use of a computer terminal or a microcomputer (plus a modem and a telecommunication program) with a computer conferencing program (usually on a mainframe computer) and telecommunications capabilities in the form of cables or phone lines.

Computer conferencing participants need not be in the same physical location or available at the same time. The computer stores their messages on receipt and makes them available to the addressees when they wish. Because of this feature, a growing number of educators have recognized the educational potential of computer conferencing for distance education (Mason and Kaye, 1989). In general, the technology can play a role in undergraduate and graduate education, business and industrial training, and informal education.

Since adult education courses frequently involve considerable discussion, computer conferencing is intuitively appealing to many professors who wish to broaden the base of student participation by accommodating the time and place constraints faced by many degree-seeking adult education students. Essentially, computer conferencing provides adult learners with a classroom that is available to them at their convenience. The various commercially available programs have features through which conference facilitators or instructors can manage the discussion much as they would in face-to-face meetings.

It is easy to imagine a somewhat similar application of computer conferencing for executive and sales training in business and industry. However, conferencing is equally useful for less formal learning, especially where discussion plays a major role and where distance, time, or other factors prevent people from gathering together physically. For example, a conference of senior citizens might have topics ranging from Social Security to Elderhostel and problems with adult children. In the true spirit of adult education, participants could choose the conference facilitator, establish any rules governing conference activities, and pick the discussion topics. Experience with SeniorNet, a computer network for elders, strongly indicates the potential success of such an effort.

Because at the present time a mainframe or minicomputer is needed to house the program, conferencing activities are now based within institutions able to afford such equipment. In the future, however, we can expect to see conferencing programs suitable for use on advanced microcomputers. We can also expect continued growth in the availability and ease of use of these computers. When these two trends converge, many more adult educators will be able to use this tool.

Computer conferencing gives teachers more flexibility than does CAIV technology. Instructors using conferencing for instruction need computer experts only for installing and maintaining the program on its host computer. Apart from that, they can function independently. In general, conferencing programs are easy to use. Even people having little computer experience quickly learn how to establish conferences (or courses), open topics, and manage their operation. Nothing about the course is locked into place by the technology. Changes are readily made and instantly implemented. Given this type of control, a teacher preferring a learner-centered, informal, collaborative approach to instruction can use that style as easily as in a face-to-face classroom discussion. A teacher preferring a more formal, directive approach can just as easily follow that style.

However, conferencing is not suitable for all types of content or all types of instructional strategies. Its forte is discussion. Also, in its current state of development, conferencing is mostly limited to text. This situation is subject to rapid change, but right now users generally cannot include much in the way of graphics in their on-line conferencing activities. Thus, some content areas may not be very suitable for computer conferencing. However, when it is an appropriate choice, it helps meet the needs of learners who otherwise cannot overcome barriers imposed by time and location. Many teachers will find the technology congenial because they retain classroom-like independence when using it.

Video. One of video's most useful functions is to serve as a pipeline for delivering instruction of all kinds—degree-oriented courses, informal leisure and recreation programs, and continuing education modules. In contrast to computer conferencing, teaching on television often involves working with an array of experts whose skills are essential for producing the quality of show expected by today's sophisticated viewer. Teachers for video-based instruction can find widely varying production conditions, ranging from well-equipped studios that include multiple cameras, sophisticated control rooms, high-quality lighting, preproduction support personnel like script writers and graphic artists, professional production crews, and postproduction editing capabilities to redesigned classrooms or other space equipped to a lesser extent and staffed with part-time crews of one or two and mixed-use space in which portable video equipment is brought in as needed. The sophisticated studio environment facilitates the creation of professional-quality productions, but even more limited systems are capable of generating videos that meet basic viewer expectations for visual and sound quality. This is very important, because decades of television viewing have created high technical expectations among audiences.

Teaching on television differs from classroom teaching in several respects, whether the production is broadcast live or from tape. For one thing, the teacher usually maintains eye contact with the camera, even if students are present during the shooting. Otherwise, viewers would never have a sense of being addressed. Also, although classroom teachers generally work from outlines or loose notes, video teachers are likely to follow scripts. This practice helps ensure smooth presentations having distinct closures, something important for viewers who do not have a chance to ask last-minute clarifying questions. Scripting serves another purpose. Because some word and sound combinations do not transmit as distinctly as others, teachers may find themselves working with script writers on phrasing and word choice.

There are other differences, too. In some instances, video cameras are in fixed positions, and the teacher is expected to operate a switcher during the presentation to choose between cameras as needed. One camera might be set to capture a head-and-shoulders shot of the teacher; another might be focused on a graphics pad. The teacher can tell which camera is live by observing a monitor or the camera's red on light. In addition to giving the presentation and thinking to switch cameras, the teacher has to remember to stay within the picture framed by the camera focused on her or him.

In cases where a production crew is present, teaching on television requires cooperation and coordination between the instructor and skilled video personnel. Even with such support, a teacher's on-camera movements have to be restricted. Too quick and unexpected a motion can take part of the teacher out of the picture because the camera operator is caught off guard. Too far a movement could even take the teacher completely out of the picture.

A teacher using various graphic materials in a lesson may also need to cue the video engineer or camera operator by means of such statements as, "As we can see from the next graphic" or "This next clip shows." Use of graphics introduces additional considerations for teachers. Television graphic standards are generally higher than those for classroom use. Any graphic material used by teachers has to conform to the standard screen height-to-width ratio, known as the *aspect ratio*. Letters and lines must be of certain sizes and thicknesses, and some colors must be avoided because they do not show up well on TV. Finally, television teachers need to be concerned with their own graphic image. Whether they choose to dress formally or informally, teachers will find that certain clothing patterns and colors do not display well.

Television teachers will also find varying possibilities for student-teacher interactions. In some cases, instructors can engage in two-way video and audio communication with students off site. The less costly two-way audio with one-way video option is often substituted. In other cases, no interaction possibilities exist at all. Sometimes, students will be present during production, thus providing some possibilities for inter-action. In still other instances, the only people present during produc-tion may be the teacher and technical personnel. For novice television teachers, the transition from traditional classroom to barren studio is particularly challenging, especially if there are also no provisions for interacting with off-site students.

Television's capacity for reaching people in large numbers is undis-puted. In addition, videotape adds a dimension of flexibility attractive to many adult learners who can conveniently use their own VCRs to attend class. However, teaching by video differs from classroom teaching in various respects and requires instructors to adjust accordingly. The degree of adjustment needed is a function of local production variables.

Teaching Styles and Technology

In reporting a recent conference on teaching and technology, DeLoughry (1989, p. A13) quotes Warren B. Martin, a senior fellow at the Carnegie Foundation for the Advancement of Teaching, as saying, "Our purpose is to try to keep teaching and technology in perspective to the end that we bring the latter—technology—into the service of the former—teaching." Surely he speaks for all educators, but reaching this goal will only come about as they become both more knowledgeable about technology and more proactive in evaluating its utility.

These are not simple steps. As illustrated in this chapter, considerable diversity exists both within and among different information technologies. Yet, there are certain common factors related to their use. For one thing, instruction is mediated rather than face to face. For another, an instructor's independence and flexibility can be affected. Last, each technology has its own particular characteristics, strengths, and weaknesses. Instructors sensitive to these factors will be better able to design instructional approaches compatible with their teaching styles.

Mediated Instruction. Technology-based instruction is essentially mediated instruction. That is, the technology is interposed between teacher and students and sometimes between students and students. Perhaps this has little import when teachers merely supplement classroom activities with, say, computer-based lessons or videotapes. However, when a technology replaces face-to-face instruction, the mediation factor is significant. Consider instructors whose normal mode of discourse in class is matter-of-fact and somewhat terse and who use body language to convey warmth and approachability. In computer-mediated conferencing instruction, these teachers need to moderate the tone of their discourse, embodying in their written messages the warmth that students cannot now see. Without eye contact and other body language clues, students may interpret matter-of-factness as indifference, coldness, or hostility. Other forms of mediated instruction pose even more difficult problems. How, for example, can a teacher preferring a democratic, collaborative teaching approach maintain that style while teaching via one-way video and audio? This is just one of many questions needing investigation. In general, relationships between various teaching styles and different forms of mediated instruction are worth exploring.

Teacher Independence. Using today's sophisticated information technology generally requires some degree of collaboration or cooperation with experts in audio and video production, computer use, and mediated-lesson design. For many teachers, adjusting to a team approach is quite taxing. Also, effective use of each medium requires accommodating its particular characteristics. Instructors accustomed to the traditional independence of classroom teaching may find the adapting of favorite materials to the production standards of a given medium an irksome process. To outsiders, such adaptations may seem trivial, but it can be hard to accept the fact that a cherished set of overheads that served so well previously do not meet basic standards for video use.

Teacher Flexibility. Some loss of teacher flexibility is closely allied to a reduction in independence. Use of technology inevitably demands longer planning timelines than many instructors are accustomed to following. Equipment and facilities often have to be scheduled and reserved for use. Schedules need to be coordinated with support personnel. Graphics intended for video transmission require more careful preparation, hence more time, in order to meet reasonable TV viewing standards. Sometimes, support materials are mailed to off-site students, which means that the items must be prepared so they reach the students on time.

In addition to demanding longer planning timelines, use of technology has other implications for instructor flexibility. Rapid response to changing conditions in the student population, quick fixes of instructional problems related to the technology, and fast revisions of lessons are virtually precluded by the nature of some technologies. Too many variables—people, equipment, costs, facilities—are involved. Research is needed to help identify and develop strategies that teachers might employ to retain maximum independence and flexibility when teaching with technology.

Technological Differences. Each technology has its own characteristics, strengths, and limitations that have to be recognized if it is to be used appropriately. For example, computer conferencing facilitates group discussion and is primarily asynchronous in nature. Video is primarily a visual medium supporting both still and motion images. CAIV combines video with the interactive potential of the computer. By knowing the specific characteristics of a technology and understanding the implications of its strengths and weaknesses, teachers will make sounder educational decisions regarding its use.

Constructing a Personal Model for the Use of Technology

Clearly, the use of technology can have effects on an instructor's preferred style—that general teaching behavior that is stable over time and across circumstances. To a large degree, however, teachers can influence the extent of any effects. In his study of technology and democracy, Arterton (1987, p. 26) reports discovering "that the largest differences in the nature, the role, and the effectiveness of political participation were rooted not in technological capacity but in the models of participation that project initiators carried in their heads."

In a similar vein, I propose that instructors construct their own "model of participation" whenever they make use of a particular technology. This activity will serve as a reminder that instructional effectiveness is rooted in how instructors use the technology, not in the technology itself. It will also aid their planning process by helping them to identify critical variables that can affect the teaching process. Such a model is necessarily personal and unique to a specific technology and its institutional environment. Because it is anchored by awareness of one's preferred teaching style and combined with pertinent knowledge about a technology, the model can help teachers use technology more effectively and influence its educational applications. The framework for a personal model of participation includes recognition of one's personal teaching style, familiarity with the medium's characteristics, knowledge of the specific circumstances for using the technology, and a sense of appropriate uses for the technology.

Like the components of all models, these elements are interrelated. Each is necessary but not sufficient to help teachers be effective, satisfied users of communications technology. The next four sections discuss the contributions made by the different elements toward a personal participation model that helps instructors take proactive steps in using technology.

Recognition of One's Teaching Style. Preliminary evidence from an ongoing research project indicates that teachers have to stop and reflect when asked about their teaching styles. This is not surprising, especially given the still somewhat amorphous nature of the concept reflected in the literature. Yet, as Hyman and Rosoff (1984, p. 36) suggest, "The term *style* leads us to refer to the actions of the teacher." With that notion as a basis and fueled by Apps' model for analysis described in Chapter Two of this volume, instructors who have given little conscious thought to their teaching styles can bring them into focus. Self-reflection, student evaluations, videotapes of one's teaching, and colleagues' observations are all worthy sources for the data needed to articulate one's teaching style.

A clear sense of teaching style can help instructors determine when and if they are willing to compromise in the face of media-imposed constraints. Through awareness of style, instructors can more readily distinguish between a compromise that threatens the integrity of their teaching and one having minor consequences. Insight into style can also illuminate any need to compensate for media shortcomings. For example, if student-teacher interaction is deemed especially valuable, then what might an instructor do to facilitate it when teaching by one-way video?

Familiarity with the Medium's Characteristics. General media characteristics include properties like sound, vision, motion, color, and interactive capabilities. Media also vary in their ability to handle time. Some can function asynchronously, meaning that in the case of computer conferencing messages can be sent and received at an individual's convenience. A telephone conference call exemplifies synchronous communication. Some media can function in real time; that is, an event transpires in the same timeframe whether it is real or simulated. If, for example, an operator in a nuclear power plant has thirty seconds in which to close a valve in an emergency, then the computer simulation would also allow only thirty seconds for the person to respond before the simulated event moves to the next level of crisis. Other media can show events in slow motion or extra-fast motion.

Characteristics can further vary within a technological family. For example, computer systems differ in their capabilities to display animation or graphics. Those with graphic capabilities differ further in the nature and quality of their displays. Familiarity with a particular medium's characteristics helps instructors evaluate its utility for the educational purpose at hand. In addition, such knowledge informs selection of instructional design strategies.

Knowledge of Specific Circumstances. Constructing an effective personal model also necessitates learning the institutional context in which the technology is used. The applicable organizational policies and procedures, union rules, and relevant hierarchical relationships all bear upon a teacher's involvement with technology. This kind of knowledge, as well as cognizance of the availability and quality of technical support personnel, facilities, and equipment, helps instructors approach their involvement with technology realistically. This knowledge also helps them judge the probability of achieving satisfactory outcomes within reasonable timelines.

Sense of Appropriate Uses. Determining the appropriate uses of a technology is a complex process that includes evaluating both media characteristics and the conditions for the use of technology just discussed. Other diverse factors ranging from pertinent learner attitudes and skills to logistical issues and questions of cost-effectiveness require consideration. But, there are two significant questions: What is the educational problem? How might it be effectively and efficiently resolved? Clear answers point to further important questions. Ultimately, when the process is followed judiciously, it helps educators apply technology appropriately.

Such a model thus provides a vehicle for gathering information about particular technologies and assessing that information in light of one's teaching style. Through awareness of personal teaching style and an understanding of technology, teachers can make sounder, more professional judgments related to its use. These in turn have an empowering effect that can help educators be proactive when they employ technology. As a result, technology truly serves teachers in meeting the needs of students.

Summary

Adult educators have new opportunities to enlarge the scope of their activities through information or communications technology. However, the use of such technology raises many questions, including ones about the effects on instructors' preferred teaching styles. Although little research has been done in this area, experience indicates that teachers sometimes will find it necessary to adjust their teaching styles when using technology. At the same time, those who respond proactively in such circumstances will better direct the technology and have it serve their needs and the needs of their students. Constructing a personal participation model can help instructors reach this goal.

References

Arterton, F. C. *Teledemocracy: Can Technology Protect Democracy?* Newbury Park, Calif.: Sage, 1987.

Brand, S. *The Media Lab: Inventing the Future at M.I.T.* New York: Viking, 1987.

DeLoughry, T. J. "A Shield from the 'Dazzle Effect.'" *Chronicle of Higher Education*, March 8, 1989, p. A13.

Donnelly, W. J. *The Confetti Generation: How the New Communication Technologies are Fragmenting America.* New York: Holt, 1986.

Harasim, L. "Teaching and Learning On-Line: Issues in Computer-Mediated Graduate Courses." *Canadian Journal of Educational Communication*, 1987, *16* (2), 117–135.

Hyman, R., and Rosoff, B. "Matching Learning and Teaching Styles: The Jug and What's in It." *Theory into Practice*, 1984, *23* (1), 35–43.

McCreary, E. K., and Van Duren, J. "Educational Applications of Computer Conferencing." *Canadian Journal of Educational Communication*, 1987, *16* (2), 117–135.

Mason, R., and Kaye, A. (eds.). *Mindweave: Computers, Communication, and Distance Education.* Oxford: Pergamon, 1989.

Vallee, J. *Computer Message Systems.* New York: McGraw-Hill, 1984.

Barbara M. Florini is associate professor of adult education at Syracuse University and affiliated with the Kellogg Project there. She has a special interest in information and communication technology in relation to adult education.

What are the implications of new perspectives on women's learning for the enhancement of teaching styles?

Insights from Women's Experiences for Teaching and Learning

Elisabeth Hayes

> *In the end we found that, in our attempt to bring forward the ordinary voice, that voice had educated us.*
> —Belenky, Clinchy, Goldberger, and Tarule,
> *Women's Ways of Knowing*

Women are increasingly seeking a voice in continuing education. Participation statistics indicate that over the fifteen-year period from 1969 to 1984, the proportion of female students in continuing education programs rose from 48 percent to 53 percent (Hill, 1986). Due to this growth in numbers alone, it is increasingly important for continuing educators to understand and serve the needs and interests of female students. While considerable stress has been placed on the need for support services, such as provision of childcare, flexible scheduling, and changes in course content (Lewis, 1988), continuing educators have directed less attention toward changes in teaching strategies. However, new scholarship on women has raised questions about the assumptions and effectiveness of traditional methods of education and led to the development of an alternative approach to teaching. This approach, generally

E. R. Hayes (ed.). *Effective Teaching Styles.*
New Directions for Continuing Education, no. 43. San Francisco: Jossey-Bass, Fall 1989.

described as *feminist pedagogy*, emphasizes a collaborative, participatory teaching-learning process that engages learners in the creation of knowledge based on personal experience that can be used as the basis for individual change and social action.

Feminist pedagogy has been proposed as a particularly effective way to approach women as students and women's experiences as subject matter; in addition, it can provide continuing educators with a new perspective on appropriate teaching styles for both women and men. While many of the strategies incorporated into feminist pedagogy are similar to those associated with other humanistic and radical educational approaches, in feminist pedagogy the use of these strategies are linked to a new understanding of learner needs and societal values and thus to a new conception of desirable goals for the educational process.

In this chapter, I describe the rationale for the development of feminist pedagogy and identify some key elements that characterize this approach. This model of feminist pedagogy is a synthesis based on a number of sources and my own perceptions of salient elements. While a generally consistent overall picture of feminist pedagogy emerges from descriptions of its practice, there is considerable variation in emphasis on different elements. In addition, feminist pedagogy as a teaching style is continually evolving, along with the scholarship on women and women's education. Such an evolution is appropriate and consistent with the orientation of its advocates toward a continual process of theory development and change.

A Rationale for Feminist Pedagogy

Feminist pedagogy rests on two basic assumptions: that all the educational needs of women are not met in the most effective way through traditional models of education and that education must serve as a means for individual development and social change in order to meet these needs. A brief exploration of the origins of these assumptions may be useful as a foundation for a discussion of strategies that comprise the approach.

Part of the rationale for feminist pedagogy lies in the growing scholarship that has illuminated certain needs and characteristics of women. Gilligan (1982), Baker-Miller (1986), and others suggest that developing and maintaining caring relationships with others are central concerns for many women. These concerns have an impact on women's patterns of individual development and thus on their orientation to educational experiences as well as on the ways in which they interact with others in educational settings. The research of Belenky, Clinchy, Goldberger, and Tarule (1986) indicates that the centrality of relationships has an impact on women's intellectual development and suggests that a central issue for women as learners is developing a "voice." These researchers found that women expressed a particular need to find their own means of self-expression and to have it reaffirmed through the process of education; this need was linked to the women's prior tendency to define themselves in terms of their relationships to others. An important aspect of developing a new sense of identity for women was maintaining a balance between autonomy and interdependence with others. In accomplishing this, women indicated a preference for a process of "connected learning" emphasizing a search for connections between personal experience and new ideas, between themselves and other participants in the learning activity (Tarule, 1988).

Further, this orientation toward developing and maintaining caring relationships is reflected in women's characteristic modes of interaction:

> Women students enter the educational setting with well-developed abilities to hold their opinion silent while they question another person about hers (interviewing); to engage in narrative conversations that trace the details ("Then he said; then she said"); and to remain sensitive to how well a message is being received by checking with the listener (such as by using a tag question at the end of a statement: "Did that make sense to you?") [Tarule, 1988, p. 21].

All-women groups tend to exhibit cooperative patterns of interaction characterized by efforts to include all group members in discussion, active listening, self-disclosure, and mutual elaboration of discussion topics (Coates, 1986).

These particular learning needs and social behaviors may put women at a disadvantage in many educational settings. Traditional styles of teaching tend to foster classroom interactions that reflect competitive rather than cooperative patterns. Individual efforts to assert and defend points of view are typically more valued than listening and supporting the ideas of others. Effective participation in classroom discussions may demand the ability to engage in competitive debates and arguments over ideas rather than in cooperative dialogue. Women's preferences for more supportive interactions may make them less adept or less willing to participate in these situations; they may thus be evaluated by teacher, peers, and even by themselves as generally less competent learners. In addition, these situations may not give women the opportunity to express themselves, to have the value of their ideas recognized, to develop a voice. In contrast, a teaching style that supports cooperative dialogue and provides opportunities to explore relationships among multiple perspectives and ideas may be needed to promote an educational climate more appropriate for women.

Further, in these studies of women's development and social behavior,

women's interpersonal orientations and responsive qualities are concep-
tualized not as weaknesses but as strengths. This work gives us a new
appreciation of women's abilities to develop caring, supportive relationships and the value of such relationships for promoting individual learning and development. Thus, an alternative teaching style is not seen as
a way to accommodate women's deficiencies but rather as a model based
on new conceptions of positive personal growth. This style does not
simply accommodate differences; it supports and enhances learners'
abilities to develop positive interpersonal relationships and engage in
cooperative dialogue. In essence, the emphasis of the educational process
is shifted, and teaching strategies are selected to reflect this emphasis
(Shrewsbury, 1987).

Recent scholarship on women has clarified the ways in which
previous curriculum, theory, and research have excluded or distorted
women's experiences. Further, linked to the recognition of the limitations of prior male-based scholarship is an appreciation of the potential
limitations of any single perspective; feminist scholarship emphasizes
"a conceptualization of knowledge as a comparison of multiple perspectives leading towards a complex and evolving view of reality. Each
new contribution reflects the perspective of the person giving it; each
has something to offer" (Maher, 1985, p. 33). This orientation suggests
that appreciation of multiple perspectives and the changing nature of
knowledge is preferable to a vision of truth as absolute and objective.
Accordingly, feminist approaches to education have emphasized the
need for students to question previous assumptions and to use their
experiences and those of others to generate new understandings of the
world.

Finally, feminist pedagogy rests on the assumption that educational
benefits cannot be fully realized unless learners apply new knowledge to
make changes in their own lives and in society. In its broadest sense,
feminist pedagogy is a form of "liberating education": "education that
implies social transformation and that is designed to find answers to
fundamental social issues" (Law and Sissons, 1985, p. 69). Ongoing
inequities experienced by women form a compelling rationale for a need
for such change and for education that supports both questioning and
the search for answers.

Thus, women's concern for relationships and strength in supportive
interaction provide the basis for a teaching style that emphasizes cooperation and collaboration. The incongruency between women's experiences
and the traditional curriculum suggests the need for a teaching approach
that provides opportunities for students to "draw on their personal and
intellectual experiences to build a satisfying version of the subject, one
that they can use productively in their own lives" (Maher, 1985, p. 30).
Finally, recognition of past and present social inequities indicates that

the educational process should enhance learners' abilities to engage in efforts toward social change.

Ultimately, the rationale for feminist pedagogy lies not only in its potential to better meet the particular needs of women; there is also the assumption that this style of teaching can provide a learning environment appropriate for women and men. A view of women's characteristics and values as strengths suggests that men as well as women can benefit from an educational approach that enables learners to support each other in a mutual process of personal development and learning.

Feminist Pedagogy: Process

While there is no standard model of a feminist teaching style, a number of common elements can be identified in descriptions of feminist pedagogy. These elements include collaboration in teaching and learning, cooperative communication styles, a holistic approach to learning, strategies for theory building, and action projects. While feminist pedagogy was initially applied in the context of women's studies programs, the approach has now been used with a variety of subjects in diverse instructional settings (Bunch and Pollack, 1983).

Collaboration in Teaching and Learning. A collaborative process is at the heart of feminist pedagogy. A collaborative course structure includes the mutual planning, conducting, and evaluating of learning activities and outcomes. This type of process is considered essential for the development of a community of learners who can assume responsibility for their own growth and development as well as assist in the growth and development of others (Shrewsbury, 1987). Ideally, collaboration should exist both between instructor and students and among students as a group. The role of instructor as a collaborator in the learning process is a familiar one in the literature on continuing education, and there is a great deal of literature directed toward enhancing teachers' abilities to adopt such a role. For example, see Conti in Chapter One of this volume.

While the importance of carefully planning strategies to support collaborative learning among students is also recognized as desirable, it has received somewhat less attention in continuing education. At times it seems to be taken for granted that, given the opportunity, adult learners will find it easy to plan and engage in collaborative learning activities with other learners. However, as many educators have realized through experience with such activities, the process is not simple or spontaneous.

The nature of a collaborative learning activity is important to clarify; it is not simply an activity that is completed by a group. For an activity to be truly collaborative, the contribution of all individuals to the attainment of goals must be necessary and valued. Every student must take responsibility for the learning of every member of the learning group as well as her or his own. Clearly, in group learning activities this sense of shared responsibility often does not evolve naturally. It is necessary, particularly with individuals not accustomed to this learning format, to provide appropriate structure. Individuals must share a group goal, and efforts must be made to equalize the contribution that each member can make toward attainment of that goal. Schneidewind (1983, 1987) describes several approaches to designing collaborative learning groups that exemplify these characteristics. In one approach, which she calls the "jigsaw," each student is assigned essential information, such as part of a course reading. The students summarize important points for the rest of the group. The group then undertakes an activity that requires use of the entire reading. More examples of ways to structure collaborative groups are described by Johnson and Johnson (1975).

The collaborative process demands that both students and teachers use certain skills that are not always necessary with traditional teaching methods. As experience and common sense suggest, learners are not always able or willing initially to engage in such a process on an equal basis. Enhancing learners' abilities to learn together cooperatively is in fact an integral aspect of feminist pedagogy. Such skills are valued not only for their utility in the enhancement of content learning. From a feminist perspective, collaborative teaching and learning reflects a value placed on supportive interpersonal relationships, provides increased opportunity for learners to be exposed to multiple perspectives, and ultimately enhances skills that may be applied outside the classroom in cooperative efforts toward social change.

Cooperative Communication Styles. The success of a collaborative teaching-learning process is partly dependent on patterns of communication and interpersonal interaction. Typical patterns of classroom interaction reflect domination by the instructor or individual students. Competitive behavior can exist even in ostensibly cooperative groups when some individuals exert greater control of discussion topics and ignore or discourage the contribution of other group members.

In contrast, the collaborative process model of feminist pedagogy requires a more cooperative style of interaction. This mode can be characterized by active support for group members. Identification of elements particularly characteristic of talk in all-women groups has been helpful to clarify the nature of such a style. In these groups, speakers typically recognize and build on each others' contributions to the topic of discussion. Turn taking is encouraged through each speaker's use of questions. Active listening strategies are used to support the contributions of others.

This style demands that the instructor and learners become sensitive to the typical patterns of classroom talk and interaction and that they attempt to alter them. As with collaborative learning techniques, communication skills may need to be taught explicitly. It can be quite difficult to change habitual ways of behaving in group situations, but fairly simple strategies can be used to promote equitable contributions to discussion. For example, each individual may be given a specified number of turns to speak in a given situation. For more elaborate analysis, an observer can be assigned to take notes on classroom interaction patterns of students and instructor and then to report the observations to the entire group. This process can be used to identify inequities in communication as well as effective participation.

Patterns of cooperative communication reflect respect for others and thus support the development of trust and openness to new ideas. Because of an emphasis on sharing personal opinions and experiences in feminist pedagogy—both as a part of enhancing individual self-understanding and as a means to foster appreciation for diversity—a climate of mutual respect is essential.

Holistic Approach to Learning. Feminist pedagogical strategies are intended to support affective as well as cognitive learning, personal insight as well as skill acquisition and content knowledge. Traditional educational practices often focus primarily on cognitive learning, making affective learning, if even considered, a secondary outcome. In the feminist approach, expressing and understanding one's emotions are perceived to be critical parts of the learning process. This concern with affective learning has been traced to the roots of feminist pedagogy in the practices of consciousness-raising groups (Fisher, 1987). In these groups, the sharing of feelings was an important way to build group solidarity and illuminate shared experiences of powerlessness.

Since emotions can inhibit constructive action or be a source of energy and motivation, gaining control over one's emotional responses can be a critical means to enhance learning and ability to engage in productive activity. Fisher (1987) suggests that reflection on emotions can facilitate the process of clarifying beliefs and values. She describes a number of collaborative strategies for the exploration of how emotional responses reflect underlying understandings and judgments about course topics. Several strategies involve the group enactment of a prepared or improvised scene or play with the goal of both expressing and analyzing the feelings of individual characters.

The integrative journal, described by Berry and Black (1987), is another strategy for fostering both affective and cognitive learning. In this approach to journal writing, students are asked to make a number of different kinds of entries. Some entries are geared toward the description of personal opinions and feelings, while others consist of summaries and critiques of course material. The more innovative types of entries are integrative entries, in which students are asked to apply course concepts to current problems; dialogic entries, in which students can pose questions to instructors; and evaluative entries, which require students to assess and reflect on their other entries. Berry and Black (1987) emphasize that periodic feedback and evaluation of journals are important to promote student learning and establish the importance of the activity. This is an important point for the success of all activities used to support affective learning. Instructors can inadvertently devalue affective learning outcomes by neglecting to give as much care and attention to them as to more cognitively oriented work. Instructor evaluation of personal feelings and experiences is certainly inappropriate, but students' depth of analysis and critical reflection can be an object for instructor feedback. In this way, such activities are not simply therapeutic but rather significant ways to foster learners' thinking skills.

Strategies for Theory Building. A fourth aspect of feminist pedagogy is theory building. This element has its origins in the initial need for feminist teachers to address the exclusion or distortion of women's experiences in the content of many academic disciplines. Women's studies classes became opportunities to create new knowledge about women through the sharing and analyzing of the experiences of participants. The ongoing emphasis on theory building in feminist pedagogy reflects the assumption that all knowledge is relative, dynamic, and limited. Thus, the process of critiquing existing ideas in relation to experience and constructing new theory must be ongoing.

Theory building, according to Bunch (1983), includes several stages: description, analysis, vision, and strategy. The process begins with a consideration of multiple perspectives on a problem or issue that draws extensively on the learners' experiences when possible. Following this descriptive stage are attempts to understand why the current situation exists—the possible economic, political, biological, ecological, sociological, and other explanations. In conjunction with the feminist orientation toward individual and social change, the next step of vision is the development of goals for the attainment of alternative, more desirable realities. Finally, the cycle is completed by the development of strategies for change.

Seeing themselves as theory builders often demands a considerable change in perspective for students and perhaps even for teachers. Haywoode and Scanlon (1987, p. 106) point out that in theory building, unequal relationships among students, as well as between students and teacher, must be eliminated: "Theory building is an inherently egalitarian activity because each student may theorize about her own experience." As a result of the process, learners gain a belief in the importance of their own ideas and experiences. They must also begin to adopt an active, critical stance toward existing knowledge.

I have found role play techniques to be particularly useful to support the process of theory building. For example, in a graduate course on feminism in adult education, the class struggled with new and at times complex concepts in feminist theory through most of the semester. The ideas quite often generated strong personal reactions among the students, which they were eager to discuss. However, my coinstructor and I found it difficult to push the students beyond discussions of personal experiences to an analysis of their relation to the concepts and theory in the readings. As one course activity, we planned to develop and enact role play situations to illustrate some particularly significant issues. As a group, the class developed several scenes based on their actual experiences, and we devoted a portion of several class sessions to acting out the scenes in an improvisational fashion. After a scene was acted out, actors were asked questions about the reasons for their actions and their feelings in character. Taking the roles of other individuals forced students to go beyond their own personal perspective on issues and gave them new insight into the behavior of other people. This distancing made it easier to connect experiences to general concepts discussed in the readings. Further, presenting issues as real-life situations made it easier for learners to clarify their own values and beliefs, identify the weaknesses and strengths of existing theory, and understand how theory might be used as a guide for their own actions.

Bunch (1983) and Thompson (1987) describe additional activities that can be used to foster theory building. Common to these and other descriptions of the theory-building process is a stress on the value of learning the process as well as its outcomes. Students "become familiar with a process for ongoing reevaluation of their lives and work in light of their assumptions about women, change, and their own goals and values" (Schneidewind, 1987, p. 25).

Action Projects. Freire's (1968) concept of praxis—the integration of theory and action—is often cited in discussions of feminist education. In feminist education, as in Freire's work, the educational process is not considered complete unless learners take concrete steps to apply what is learned toward change. Action itself is seen as an educational process, an opportunity for testing and developing new theory.

While some authors have indicated difficulty in incorporating action projects into traditional college curriculum, it may be easier to include such projects in continuing education where educational programs are typically linked closely to work, family, community, or other concerns. What may be more difficult is to ensure that students are connecting theory to practice and that the action is directed toward change. Examples of this form of action project are Haywoode and Scanlon's (1987) examples from a college program for working-class women. In one example, students interviewed community members to investigate why parents were sending their children to parochial rather than public school. The class used its findings to gain an understanding of how educational institutions serve not only to provide education but also to support a stratified society. This understanding formed the basis for the generation of theory about the role of education in society. Still further, this led to increased involvement by the students in local educational affairs in an attempt to change negative perceptions of the public school.

As the authors just cited point out, integration of action projects with theory-building strategies enabled students to understand and evaluate their experience in the community critically in relation to broader concepts and provided the impetus for further community activities. In general, the combining of fieldwork with seminar discussions is an effective way to promote this process. The element of risk involved as students test ideas in the real world makes it essential that the instructor provide emotional support as well as a model for critical reflection on action.

Feminist Pedagogy in Practice

These elements—collaboration in teaching and learning, cooperative communication styles, a holistic approach to learning, strategies for theory building, and action projects—are not unique to feminist pedagogy. What is unique is the reconsideration of the value of such strategies in light of their relationship to women's needs as learners and an appreciation of women's strengths and experiences. Ultimately, too, feminist pedagogy suggests more than a set of teaching strategies. As Fisher (1987, pp. 55–56) states: "In its most important sense, feminist pedagogy concerns understanding and vision, not teaching tricks." Such understanding includes an attempt to understand all students' perspectives and to understand the limitations of our own. Vision includes continually striving to see beyond the limitations of our students, ourselves, and our society and establishing educational goals that will assist students and ourselves to overcome these limitations.

As a teaching style, it may be most consistently reflected in the nature of our own relationships as educators with our students. Noddings (1986) characterizes such relationships as based on an ethic of care. In these relationships, the teacher acts out of a sense of direct responsibility to individual learners, not professional duty. As teachers, we convey care for individuals through our confirmation of their present strengths and future potential and through our concern for their personal growth in a broad sense.

Such relationships, and feminist pedagogy, are a model not only for the education of women in a certain context but for all teachers and learners. Perhaps the most important insight from recent scholarship is that both men and women are limited by traditional sex role stereotypes and that everyone might benefit from education based on an expanded conception of positive personal growth and ways of learning. As teachers, we may benefit as well from a perspective on teaching that allows us to appreciate and utilize the strengths of all learners and to see our teaching in a broad scope that includes visions of a changed society.

References

Baker-Miller, J. B. *Toward a New Psychology of Women.* Boston: Beacon Press, 1986.

Belenky, M. F., Clinchy, B. M., Goldberger, N. R., and Tarule, J. M. *Women's Ways of Knowing.* New York: Basic Books, 1986.

Berry, E., and Black, E. "The Integrative Learning Journal." *Women's Studies Quarterly,* 1987, *15* (3-4), 59-64.

Bunch, C. "Not By Degrees: Feminist Theory and Education." In C. Bunch and S. Pollack (eds.), *Learning Our Way: Essays in Feminist Education.* Trumansburg, N.Y.: Crossing Press, 1983.

Bunch, C., and Pollack, S. (eds.). *Learning Our Way: Essays in Feminist Education.* Trumansburg, N.Y.: Crossing Press, 1983.

Coates, J. *Women, Men, and Language.* London: Longman, 1986.

Fisher, B. "The Heart Has Its Reasons: Feelings, Thinking, and Community Building in Feminist Education." *Women's Studies Quarterly,* 1987, *15* (3-4), 47-58.

Freire, P. *Pedagogy of the Oppressed.* New York: Seabury Press, 1968.

Gilligan, C. *In a Different Voice: Psychological Theory and Women's Development.* Cambridge, Mass.: Harvard University Press, 1982.

Haywoode, T. L., and Scanlon, L. P. "World of Our Mothers: College for Neighborhood Women." *Women's Studies Quarterly,* 1987, *15* (3-4), 101-109.

Hill, S. *Trends in Adult Education 1969-1984.* Washington, D.C.: Center for Education Statistics, 1986.

Johnson, D., and Johnson, R. *Learning Together and Alone: Cooperation, Competition, and Individualization.* Englewood Cliffs, N.J.: Prentice-Hall, 1975.

Law, M., and Sissons, L. "Involving Adults in Social Change Education." In S. H. Rosenblum (ed.), *Involving Adults in the Educational Process.* New Directions for Continuing Education, no. 26. San Francisco: Jossey-Bass, 1985.

Lewis, L. H. (ed.). *Addressing the Needs of Returning Women.* New Directions for Continuing Education, no. 39. San Francisco: Jossey-Bass, 1988.

Maher, F. "Classroom Pedagogy and the New Scholarship on Women." In *Gendered Subjects: The Dynamics of Feminist Teaching.* Boston: Routledge & Kegan Paul, 1985.

Noddings, N. "Fidelity in Teaching, Teacher Education, and Research for Teaching." *Harvard Educational Review,* 1986, *56* (4), 496-510.

Schneidewind, N. "Feminist Values: Guidelines for a Teaching Methodology in Women's Studies." In C. Bunch and S. Pollack (eds.), *Learning Our Way: Essays in Feminist Education.* Trumansburg, N.Y.: Crossing Press, 1983.

Schneidewind, N. "Teaching Feminist Process." *Women's Studies Quarterly,* 1987, *15* (3-4), 15-31.

Shrewsbury, C. M. "What Is Feminist Pedagogy?" *Women's Studies Quarterly,* 1987, *15* (3-4), 6-14.

Tarule, J. M. "Voices of Returning Women." In L. H. Lewis (ed.), *Addressing the Needs of Returning Women.* New Directions for Continuing Education, no. 39. San Francisco: Jossey-Bass, 1988.

Thompson, M. "Diversity in the Classroom: Creating Opportunities for Learning Feminist Theory." *Women's Studies Quarterly,* 1987, *15* (3-4), 81-89.

Elisabeth Hayes is assistant professor of adult education at Syracuse University. She has developed and taught a graduate course on feminism and adult education, and her research interests include an emphasis on gender issues in adult education.

*Teaching style and the classroom social environment interact
in complex ways.*

Enhancing the Adult Classroom Environment

Gordon G. Darkenwald

This chapter examines the social environment of the adult classroom as
it relates to teacher behavior or style. *Classroom* is used here to refer to
any organized group learning situation, such as workshops, conferences,
or training programs. Teaching style is conceived as a set of preferred or
characteristic behaviors in which a teacher engages for the purpose of
promoting student learning.

The Classroom Environment

The concept of social environment or climate has been metaphorically
defined (Moos, 1979) as the personality of a classroom or other social
group. Literally, the social environment is created by the characteristics
and interactions of students and teacher. Since these characteristics and
interactions vary, no two classes can ever be exactly alike. This is
especially true of adult classes, in which experience-related diversity is
accentuated.

Social climate, though primary, is not the only condition that varies.
Others that also affect learning outcomes include subject matter; students'
prior knowledge, experience, and ability; institutional constraints; support services; and facilities.

E. R. Hayes (ed.). *Effective Teaching Styles.*
New Directions for Continuing Education, no. 43. San Francisco: Jossey-Bass, Fall 1989.

Relation to Teaching Styles

If, as social environment theory postulates, behavior is mainly the result of person-environment interactions, then understanding effective teaching styles necessitates a social-environmental perspective that includes recognition of the importance of person-environment fit for student satisfaction and achievement. Furthermore, teachers need to be aware that their effectiveness requires a flexible repertoire of teaching behaviors that they can draw on selectively as conditions vary. Aside from subject matter ignorance, lack of responsiveness and disorganization have been repeatedly identified as key behaviors associated with ineffective teaching practice.

An important question is whether, in general, the teacher or students exert primary control over the nature of learning environments. Moos (1980, p. 246) concluded from a review of secondary school social climate research that "teachers are somewhat more important in creating classroom learning environments than students are." This makes intuitive sense, for high school curricula are relatively fixed, which puts pressure on the teacher to dispense the prescribed knowledge to students and to resist any attempts at diversion. Moreover, schoolchildren and teachers are not age-status peers, a fact that profoundly affects equality and reciprocity in social relations in school settings.

In the case of continuing education, age-status equality exerts a press toward greater student influence on the nature of the learning environment, as do many other characteristics of adult students and the fact that they are typically voluntary learners.

In a Swedish study of adult education teachers' conceptions of teaching, Larsson (1983, p. 355) found that the adult students' conceptions "of teaching were perceived as the dominant restrictions on the teachers' actions. . . . Many teachers regarded this as a question of control over the educational process."

What is most important, however, is not the matter of relative influence over the learning climate but awareness by teachers that they and their adult students are mutually obligated to create optimal conditions for learning. A cardinal principle of effective teaching, therefore, is that the teacher takes the necessary actions to see that these mutual obligations are brought to fruition. This principle is not a veiled prescription for a learner-centered or "andragogical" teaching style. In many circumstances, optimal conditions for learning require a directive or subject-centered configuration of teacher behaviors.

Measuring Adult Classroom Environments

The research reported in this chapter was conducted by the author and his doctoral students at Rutgers University. Our theoretical and methodological assumptions were based on the work of Rudolf Moos, the leading researcher on classroom environments in school settings (1979). However, an initial exploratory study (Darkenwald and Gavin, 1987), which employed Moos's Classroom Environment Scale (CES) (Trickett and Moos, 1973), led us to conclude that the CES was invalid for assessing adult classroom climates. Consequently, the Adult Classroom Environment Scale (ACES) was developed before any further research was undertaken.

Like the CES, the ACES conceptualizes the classroom environment "as a dynamic social system that includes not only teacher behavior and teacher-student interaction but also student-student interaction" (Moos, 1979, p. 138). The ACES measures seven empirically based dimensions that describe a positive or growth-enhancing adult learning environment. A detailed theoretical and technical discussion of the instrument's development can be found in Darkenwald (1987).

Briefly, the scale, which is self-administered, consists of forty-nine items, seven items for each of seven dimensions (see Exhibit 1). Both total and subscale scores can be computed, depending on the purpose of the research. Two forms were produced: Actual and Ideal. The actual form refers to perceptions of the "real" or enacted environment. In contrast, the Ideal form assesses how respondents characterize their preferred classroom environment. The two forms contain identical items but different directions. Either form can be administered to both teachers and students.

Table 1 gives definitions for each ACES dimension as well as sample items. Exhibit 1 contains the full-scale items organized by the seven dimensions.

Dimensions Stressing Teaching Style

The seven ACES dimensions vary greatly in the extent to which they emphasize teacher behaviors or components of teaching style. The Involvement and Affiliation subscales contain no items that refer to teacher behavior. In contrast, all seven items that comprise the Teacher Support and the Organization and Clarity dimensions tap aspects of teaching style. Student Influence and Personal Goal Attainment contain four and three teacher behavior items respectively. Task Orientation contains one. In interpreting the research findings presented here, the degree to which each subscale taps teacher behavior should be kept in mind.

Research Findings

Most of the findings of the first major study to employ ACES have been published elsewhere (Darkenwald, 1987). However, given that study's relevance to the topic of this chapter, they bear further discussion. For a detailed account of the methodology of the study, see the article just

Exhibit 1. Adult Classroom Environment Scale Items

Involvement

Students are often bored in the class. (–)

Students often ask the teacher questions.

Most students enjoy the class.

Most students look forward to the class.

Most students in the class pay attention to what the teacher is saying.

Most students take part in class discussions.

A few students dominate the discussions in class. (–)

Affiliation

Students often share their personal experiences during class.

The students in the class work well together.

The students in the class learn little from one another. (–)

The students in the class enjoy working together.

Students in the class feel free to disagree with one another.

Friendships have developed in the class.

Students seldom interact with one another during class. (–)

Teacher Support

The teacher makes little effort to help students succeed. (–)

The teacher talks down to students. (–)

The teacher encourages students to do their best.

The teacher cares about students' feelings.

The teacher respects students as individuals.

The teacher likes the students in the class.

The teacher cares whether or not the students learn.

Task Orientation

The teacher seldom talks about things not related to the course.

Students regularly meet assignment deadlines.

Students often discuss things not related to course content. (–)

Activities not related to course objectives are kept to a minimum.

Students do a lot of work in the class.

Getting work done is very important in the class.

The class is more a social hour than a place to learn. (–)

Personal Goal Attainment

The class is flexible enough to meet the needs of individual students.

Many students think the class is not relevant to their lives. (-)

The teacher expects every student to learn the exact same things. (-)

Students in the class can select assignments that are of personal interest to them.

Most students in the class achieve their personal learning goals.

The teacher tries to find out what individual students want to learn.

Students have the opportunity to learn at their own pace.

Organization and Clarity

The teacher comes to class prepared.

Learning objectives were made clear at the start of the course.

The class is well organized.

The class lacks a clear sense of direction. (-)

The subject matter is adequately covered.

Students do not know what is expected of them. (-)

Learning activities follow a logical sequence.

Student Influence

Students help to decide the topics to be covered in class.

The teacher makes all the decisions in the class. (-)

The teacher sticks to the lesson plan regardless of student interest. (-)

Students participate in setting course objectives.

The teacher rarely dominates classroom discussion.

Students feel free to question course requirements.

The teacher seldom insists that you do things his or her way.

Note: Items denoted (-) are reverse scored.

Table 1. Dimensions and Subscales

Scale	Scale Description	Sample Item
Involvement (INV)	Extent to which students are satisfied with class and participate actively and attentively in activities	Most students take part in class discussions. (+)
Affiliation (AFF)	Extent to which students like and interact positively with each other	Students seldom interact with one another during class. (−)
Teacher Support (SUPT)	Extent of help, encouragement, concern, and friendship that teacher directs toward students	The teacher cares about students' feelings. (+)
Task Orientation (TSK)	Extent to which students and teacher maintain focus on task and value achievement	The class is more a social hour than a place to learn. (−)
Personal Goal Attainment (PGA)	Extent to which teacher is flexible, providing opportunities for students to pursue their individual interests	The teacher expects every student to learn the exact same things. (−)
Organization and Clarity (ORG)	Extent to which class activities are clear and well organized	The teacher comes to class prepared. (+)
Student Influence (INFL)	Extent to which teacher is learner-centered and allows students to participate in course planning decisions	Students participate in setting objectives. (+)

Note: Items designated (+) are scored 1, 2, 3, and 4 respectively for the responses Strongly Disagree, Disagree, Agree, Strongly Agree. Items designated (−) are scored in the reverse manner.

cited. In brief, the data were obtained from adults in credit classes in a community college in a depressed area ($n = 308$), an evening M.B.A. program in a large Pennsylvania university ($n = 156$), and a large adult school in a middle-class community ($n = 266$). The findings are depicted graphically in Figure 1.

By comparing the profiles for the Student Ideal and Student Actual ratings shown in Figure 1, we can gauge the kind of classroom environment that adult students want and compare it with what they see as the reality. What students want most is a learning environment characterized by Involvement, Teacher Support, Task Orientation, and Organization and Clarity. What students actually encounter, however, is a social climate deficient in all these attributes. For all seven ACES dimensions, the differences between Student Ideal and Student Actual ratings were statistically significant beyond the .05 level.

**Figure 1. ACES Form A and Form I Profiles
for Students and Teachers in Fifty-Five Classrooms**

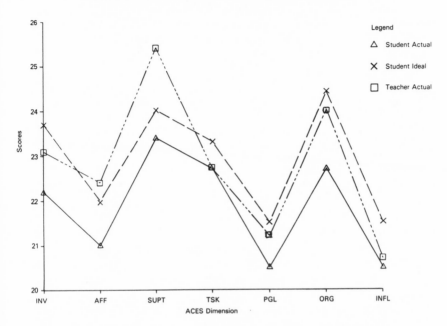

Figure 1 also reveals a pattern of discrepancies between students' and teachers' ratings of the actual or enacted classroom social environment. With the exception of Task Orientation and Student Influence, the differences in scale ratings were statistically significant.

In general, teachers perceive the classroom environment as more positive or growth-enhancing than do students. Since students' assessments of the classroom environment are more valid than those of individual teachers (Moos, 1979), one can only conclude that the majority of teachers do not know how their students experience the classroom social environment. This lack of awareness could very well result in less than optimal conditions for learning as well as in less than optimal outcomes.

A recent large-scale experiment suggests that awareness per se may not be enough (Sullivan, 1989). Fifty-eight community college evening credit classes with a total of 1,127 adult students were randomly assigned to control and experimental groups. The experimental group teachers received detailed feedback on discrepancies between their own and their students' Form A ratings early in the semester. It was hypothesized that the teachers receiving feedback would take some action to narrow the discrepancies, but in fact they did not. Postexperiment interviews with the experimental group teachers were revealing. For example, a large number were teaching a course for the first time. They said they were too preoccupied with "getting it all together" to make use of the feedback data. Instructors not teaching a course for the first time said they would have used the feedback had they been asked to do so. They were not asked to take any specific actions, which suggests that the feedback intervention could have been more directive.

The findings indicate that teachers may need more than feedback or awareness if they are to take action to modify classroom environments to enhance student satisfaction and learning. All the experimental group teachers stated that they found the feedback interesting, important, or even "helpful," despite the fact that they failed to make use of it.

Implications

The social environment of the classroom, as noted earlier, is strongly affected by the role of the teacher. For this reason, the ACES can be considered a measure not only of the quality of adult learning environments but of effective teaching behaviors or styles as well. Consequently, the ACES can be utilized as a tool for simultaneous evaluation of adult learning environments and teaching effectiveness. Teachers and administrators have told us that they could benefit from in-service training that used ACES to accomplish the following purposes: create awareness of students' preferred learning environments and teaching styles, identify discrepancies between students' and teachers' perceptions of actual or existing classroom social environments, find ways to involve adult students in efforts to enhance the overall quality of classroom environments, and motivate teachers to use feedback from students to improve teaching-learning transactions.

These and other staff development activities presuppose that what the ACES and its dimensions measure, and why, have been discussed and clarified and that program administrators have made a commitment to collect ACES data anonymously from teachers and students on a continuing basis.

References

Darkenwald, G. G. "Assessing the Social Environment of Adult Classes." *Studies in the Education of Adults*, 1987, *19* (2), 127–136.

Darkenwald, G. G., and Gavin, W. "Dropout as a Function of Discrepancies Between Expectations and Actual Experiences of the Classroom Social Environment." *Adult Education Quarterly*, 1987, *37* (3), 152–163.

Larsson, S. "Paradoxes in Teaching." *Instructional Science*, 1983, *12*, 355–365.

Moos, R. H. *Evaluating Educational Environments*. San Francisco: Jossey-Bass, 1979.

Moos, R. H. "Evaluating Classroom Learning Environments." *Studies in Educational Evaluation*, 1980, *6*, 239–252.

Sullivan, E. A. "Effects of Student Feedback to Teachers on the Psychosocial Environment of the Adult Classroom." Unpublished doctoral dissertation, Rutgers University, 1989.

Trickett, E. J., and Moos, R. H. "The Social Environment of Junior High and High School Classrooms." *Journal of Educational Psychology,* 1973, *65,* 93–102.

Gordon G. Darkenwald is professor of adult and continuing education, director of the Center for Adult Development at Rutgers University, and former editor-in-chief of New Directions for Continuing Education.

Teaching competence can be viewed from different perspectives according to a teacher's stage of professional development.

Three Stages of Teacher Competence: A Developmental Perspective

Daniel D. Pratt

The idea of teacher competency is complex even though the appeal of the concept of competency lies probably precisely in its seductive suggestion of simplicity. The idea of competency implies a promise that, reasonably speaking, anyone who wishes to become a teacher can acquire the skills to become one. But competency does not only refer to the more technical skills of teaching. The true significance of competency has more to do with the real meaning of the being of teaching: what a teacher is [van Manen, 1984, p. 141.].

Competence is often defined in relational terms. That is, people are not competent in and of themselves, only in relation to something else. Thus, the competence of a teacher might be judged in relation to a number of things, for example, a teacher's knowledge, performance of routines, accommodation of individual differences, ability to handle difficult situations, relationship with students, reputation with colleagues, impact on society, or effect upon student learning. Some might argue that competent teachers should accomplish all the things just mentioned.

However, most of us would say that some of the things just mentioned

E. R. Hayes (ed.). *Effective Teaching Styles.*
New Directions for Continuing Education, no. 43. San Francisco: Jossey-Bass, Fall 1989.

are more important than others. In this way, we take a stand as to what teaching means and how we should be held accountable as teachers. This chapter argues that the nature of teacher competence changes as teachers move through developmental stages and, further, that the forms of competence that define excellence in teaching are interrelated. Three stages of professional development and forms of competence in teaching are described: mastery of skills and procedures, clinical problem-solving, and critical reflection.

Stage One: Mastery of Skills and Procedures

In the initial phase of a teaching career, the usual focus for the assessment of competence is on the teacher's ability to transmit knowledge and guide learners toward specific goals. It is assumed that there is a direct and significant relationship between teacher behavior and adult learning. Competence is, therefore, defined in terms of the mastery of basic teaching skills and procedures that have been shown to correlate with learner achievement. From this perspective, three kinds of knowledge are seen as instrumental to effective teaching: content knowledge, propositional knowledge, and procedural knowledge.

The term *content knowledge* refers to skill and knowledge in a content area, and it is considered by most adult educators to be an essential and first priority for teachers. In many instances, this is the sole criterion for selecting a teacher of adults.

The term *propositional knowledge* refers to a teacher's knowledge of principles that govern adult learning. Examples include the principle of immediate confirmation of correct responses, which suggests that the main function of feedback is to reinforce a correct response, or Knowles' (1980) principles of adult learning, which are associated with his notion of andragogy. I have shown elsewhere how both of these are problematic yet persistent in the minds of those who seek a guiding set of universal principles (Pratt, 1987, 1988).

The term *procedural knowledge* refers to knowledge and skill in implementing procedures and routines that correlate with adult learning. Some of this knowledge has been popular since the 1950s, such as the use of behavioral objectives in the planning, conduct, and evaluation of learning. More recently, researchers in elementary and secondary education have provided evidence to suggest that learner performance in several subject areas can be significantly increased if the teacher follows certain procedures. The most convincing body of literature to support this view comes from mastery learning (Bloom, 1984) and direct instruction (Rosenshine and Stevens, 1986).

With adult education, this conception of competence is an unusual blend of humanistic and operant psychology. On the one hand, it emphasizes the role of teacher as facilitator and the process of education as collaborative. On the other hand, it stresses the "training" of adult educators and the transmission of knowledge from teacher to learner through a systems approach. In both cases, it espouses general principles of learning and teaching that are applicable across variations in learners and context. The focus is on the means (how to teach) with little serious examination of the ends (what will be learned).

For many adult educators, this is the most important form of competence in teaching. It is prescriptive and tells them what to do on Monday morning. However, there are problems associated with this point of view. First, research suggests that many of the recommended teaching procedures are only appropriate for well-defined content that will remain relatively stable over time, for example, mathematics, carpentry, and safety procedures. As a result, they are not well suited to content that lacks structure and a clear delineation of steps, for example, creative writing, second-language learning, and critical reasoning (Rosenshine and Stevens, 1986).

Second, it focuses too exclusively on the behavior of the teacher and in so doing neglects the significant role of reasoning. For some, the essence of teaching lies not in the acts of teaching but in the interaction between thoughtful reasoning and action (Clark and Peterson, 1986). By separating reasoning from action, we separate the decision from the actor and assume that a teacher can uncritically follow algorithms that will result in significant learning. The work of Marton, Hounsell, and Entwistle (1984) points out the fallacy of this thinking and the shallowness of learning that can result.

Third, the essential skills and knowledge of this stage are not linked by any conceptual framework. As a result, teachers at this stage often exhibit rapid closure and categorical judgment when presented with difficult situations and a limited ability to respond to unfamiliar situations. As a result, there is a tendency to misrepresent teaching as simply a repertoire of technical actions and principles.

This conception of competence in teaching is represented in such works as Dickinson (1973, 1981), Draves (1984), Guilbert (1981), Lowman (1984), Practical Management Associates (1979), Pratt (1981), Renner (1983), Stephens and Roderick (1974), and Sullivan (no date).

Stage Two: Clinical Problem Solving

In the second stage of an individual's development as a teacher, the emphasis shifts from fixed routines to flexible problem solving. This stage is characterized by the emergence of a conceptual framework that allows a teacher to be more consistent and more adaptive when confronting unpredictable situations. Knowledge related to teaching is perceived to be relative and flexible. Effective teachers construct new knowledge about teaching and learning based on their experience, existing knowledge, and what the situation demands. Research from this perspective has sought to understand how novice and expert teachers use their knowledge of learners, context, and subject matter to derive appropriate teaching roles and strategies.

At this stage, competent teachers are decision makers working within complex, highly ambiguous, and changing environments. It is expected that unclear problems will arise and that they will have serious implications for decision making. Prescribed routines and principles will not fit every case, nor is it expected that every problem will have a "right" solution. Competent teachers must be able to adapt to situations that are unpredictable and generate rational strategies that have a high probability of accomplishing desired ends. They must be able to anticipate learners' common conceptions, misconceptions, difficulties, and motivational orientations and as a result be able to transform or represent subject matter knowledge in forms and language appropriate to those learners (Wilson, Shulman, and Richert, 1987).

Each of the kinds of knowledge acquired in stage one is now held as conditional, that is, as dependent upon the context and situation. It is not sufficient to have a repertoire of techniques; effective teachers are expected to create means appropriate to the conditions of the moment. Teachers demonstrate competence of this sort when they are able to combine their knowledge of subject matter, learners, institutions, goals, and teaching methods imaginatively in order to solve problems and generate appropriate teaching roles and strategies. They go beyond the reductive stance of stage one and perceive the situation as a set of dynamic, interactive variables that require flexible and adaptive use of their existing knowledge. An example of this can be seen in research on agricultural extension workers where the most effective teachers or agents, as judged by Copa and Sandmann (1987), were those who could see both the details and the "big picture." Thus, the essential difference between stage one and stage two is in the role of conditional knowledge (Brophy, 1986); that is, the ability to use, adapt, and modify existing knowledge within new and uncertain situations.

This type of knowledge cannot be evaluated through observation alone. Complex mental processes, essential to competent practice, are not assumed to be knowable through observing a teacher's actions or by fragmenting the process of teaching into microportions. Each decision is a product of the teacher's professional judgment and can only be evaluated within the context of which it is a part. Thus, while the observable acts of teaching may look similar across situations, there may be considerable variation in the underlying rationale that led to the decision to act in a particular way. Within this stage of development, judgments about teacher competence must consider not only what was done (actions) but why it was done (rationale) and what might have been done (alternatives). In other words, a competent teacher must be able to monitor and diagnose complex, unpredictable learning situations, consider a number of alternative courses of action, and determine and execute an appropriate course of action.

However, here, too, there are problems. While there is no prescribed repertoire of skills and strategies, the focus is still on the means (how to teach). The emphasis has shifted from teacher behavior to teacher thinking, but the emphasis upon technical rationality and instrumental problem solving continues. Both approaches effectively ignore the dominant cultural values that influence choices and actions, and the second approach assumes that rational decision making can be applied to the teaching process as if it were neutral and value-free.

This perspective is represented in such works as Berliner (1987), Brookfield (1986), Calderhead (1987), Conti (1985), Daloz (1986), Entwistle (1985), Halkes and Olson (1984), Pratt (1984), Schneider-Fuhrmann and Grasha (1983), Shores (1985), and Shulman (1987).

Stage Three: Critical Reflection on Knowledge and Values

The third stage of professional development is characterized by a consideration of the relationship between social and cultural values and teachers' professional knowledge. Within this stage, it is recognized that teaching requires a flexible approach to problem solving, but there is also an awareness of cultural values that impose themselves on both ends and means—goals and strategies. Ways of thinking and acting are understood to be cultural as well as conditional. Thus, the practice of teaching is seen as embedded within the dominant culture of one's society.

This form of competence shifts the emphasis from skill development and problem solving to critical reflection on one's practice. Although critical reflection can occur within each stage of development, it is more dominant here. Stage three suggests an increased ability and willingness to reflect upon each of the elements within the teaching situation and to see them as part of larger systems of meaning. The teacher's personal construction of knowledge is seen as happening within, and subject to, cultural values and implicit theories related to learning and teaching. Competence, therefore, includes an understanding of the relationship between one's teaching and personal and cultural values and the ability to reflect critically upon that relationship.

Within this stage, professional knowledge is understood to be a combination of what teachers bring to the practice of teaching and something that they construct through reflection in action (while teaching) and reflection on action (after teaching). Both types of reflection involve an attempt to create meaning from problematic moments in practice. Schön (1983) describes the process this way:

> When we set the problem, we select what we will treat as the "things" of the situation, we set the boundaries of our attention to it, and we impose upon it a coherence [that] allows us to say what is wrong and in what directions the situation needs to be changed. Problem setting is a process in which, interactively, we name the things to which we will attend and frame the context in which we will attend to them [Schön, 1983, p. 40].

Reflection, then, is critical and oriented toward action; it is concerned with reorienting the assumptions and intentions upon which action rests. Such reflection is not simply a technique or skill, nor is it to be confused with the simple turning inward of personal introspection. It is conscious, intentional movement of critical thought back and forth between practice and ideology, between self and society, asking why and how things came to be as they are. Much less is taken for granted; everything is seen as "problematic" and as a possible source of further scrutiny and understanding. Thus, each of the elements within the teaching and learning situation is seen as embedded within larger systems of meaning.

As mentioned earlier, at this stage of development any of the elements in the teaching situation can be considered problematic, including the goals. For example, competent teachers would critically question the origin of personal, institutional, and societal goals; the effect of those goals upon the role of the teacher and the rights of learners; what cultural and societal values are reflected in the goals; and whether those implied values were congruent with the teacher's and learners' expressed purposes and needs. Here, the concern is for the social conditions in which the process of teaching and learning is conducted and the relations of power and authority that structure and influence those conditions.

One example of this form of competence is discussed by Ted Aoki (1984) of the University of Alberta. He talks about teachers working with learners to link the universal with the particular, the concrete, day-to-day world of personal action with the world of ideas, values, and symbols. He goes on to describe how a teacher ventures forth with learners in this exploration:

> The teacher in becoming involved with his students enters into their world as he allows them to enter his and engages himself with students mutually in action-reflection-oriented activities. He questions his students as well as himself as he urges students to question him and themselves. Mutual reflection allows new questions to emerge, which in turn leads to more reflection. In the ongoing process [that] is dialectical and transfor-

mative of social reality, both teacher and students become participants in open dialogue. . . . in critical reflection the everyday type of attitude is placed in "brackets," as it were, and examined in an attempt to go beyond the immediate level of interpretation. In this sense, critical reflection is thoughtful action, that is, action full of thought. Critical reflection thus leads to an understanding of what is beyond; it is oriented towards making the unconscious conscious. Such reflective activity allows liberation from the unconsciously held assumptions and intentions that lie hidden . . . critical reflection demonstrates interest in discovering the hidden "true" interests embedded in some given personal or social condition [Aoki, 1984, pp. 76-77].

In this sense, competence is grounded in more than simple congruence between intentions and actions; it requires a clarification of the relationship between society's values, one's personal beliefs, and one's intentions, actions, and judgment within a particular teaching context. At this stage of development, the ways in which a person sets problems and frames puzzling situations are understood to be intimately connected not just to pedagogical or andragogical knowledge but also to underlying and often implicit values that are acted upon unconsciously. The ability to perceive the relationship between values and problem framing is crucial to this form of competence.

This perspective is represented in such works as Apple (1984), Brookfield (1987), Carlson (1987), Fenstermacher (1978), Giroux and McLaren (1986), Greene (1986), Grimmett and Erickson (1988), Lather (1986), Mezirow (1981), Pratt (1988), and Shor (1986).

Concluding Thoughts

It is important to note that each stage of development requires some aspect of all three forms of competence. Furthermore, neither the stages of development nor the forms of competence are mutually exclusive; there are no fixed boundaries and no clear points of entry and exit. Instead, there is a progression of development and gradual shift in emphasis regarding competence in teaching. For example, the development of skills and routines within stage one should be accompanied by some concern for contextual sensitivity and critical reflectivity. Figure 1 shows a hypothetical relationship between forms of competence and stages of development.

The relative emphasis on one form of competence at each stage of development corresponds to the need and developmental readiness of the teacher.

For example, with beginning teachers or experienced practitioners who want to teach their craft, it may be most appropriate to have them

Figure 1. Stages of Development and Forms of Competence

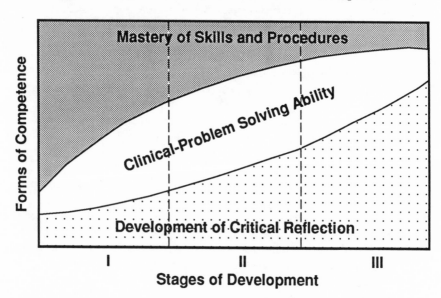

master unambiguous guidelines, skills, and procedures for getting started and to minimize critical reflection on the problematic nature of what they are doing. Such procedures and skills are the building blocks for survival in the initial phase of a teaching career and may provide the structure necessary to help novices cope with the stress and complexities of teaching.

As teachers gain experience and confidence, they may be ready to think more situationally. They are not so likely to be dependent upon fixed procedures and routines. They will be able to see beyond the morass of the particular and not only draw upon familiar routines but create new and original ones. The movement from a relatively unambiguous and structured way of thinking to contextual thinking can also suggest a readiness for more critical reflection on the embedded values that influence who they are, what they do, and why they continue to teach as they do.

With each subsequent stage of development, nothing will be as it was before. What was taken for granted at one point will become the focus of concern at another. Much of what was considered competent teaching in an earlier stage will now come under critical analysis. This means that teachers must be psychologically ready to move from one stage to the next. They must have sufficient experience, proficiency, and dissatisfaction with their current stage of development before they will be ready to move to the next stage.

Finally, the movement through stages of development and forms of competence will also involve a reconsideration of earlier learning. For, as one considers contextual variation there may be a need to reconsider basic skills, and as one examines personal and societal values, there may be a change in how one adapts to variations in context. Indeed, movement through the stages should not only change the nature of one's competence but highlight the relationships and interdependency of all three forms of competence.

References

Aoki, T. "Competence in Teaching as Instrumental and Practical Action: A Critical Analysis." In E. C. Short (ed.), *Competence: Inquiries into Its Meaning and Acquisition in Educational Settings.* Lanham, Md.: University Press of America, 1984.

Apple, M. W. "Curricular Form and the Logic of Technical Control." In E. C. Short (ed.), *Competence: Inquiries into Its Meaning and Acquisition in Educational Settings.* Lanham, Md.: University Press of America, 1984.

Berliner, D. C. "Ways of Thinking About Students and Classrooms by More and Less Experienced Teachers." In J. Calderhead (ed.), *Exploring Teachers' Thinking.* London: Cassell Educational, 1987.

Bloom, B. S. "The 2-Sigma Problem: The Search for Methods of Group Instruction as Effective as One-to-One Tutoring." *Educational Researcher,* 1984, *13,* 4–16.

Brophy, J. *Educating Teachers About Managing Classrooms and Students.* Occasional Paper no. 115. East Lansing: Institute for Research on Teaching, Michigan State University, 1986.

Brookfield, S. D. *Understanding and Facilitating Adult Learning: A Comprehensive Analysis of Principles and Effective Practices.* San Francisco: Jossey-Bass, 1986.

Brookfield, S. D. *Developing Critical Thinkers: Challenging Adults to Explore Alternative Ways of Thinking and Acting.* San Francisco: Jossey-Bass, 1987.

Calderhead, J. (ed.). *Exploring Teachers' Thinking.* London: Cassell Educational, 1987.

Carlson, D. "Teachers as Political Actors: From Reproductive Theory to the Crisis of Schooling." *Harvard Educational Review,* 1987, *57* (3), 283–307.

Clark, C., and Peterson, P. L. "Teachers' Thought Processes." In M. C. Wittrock (ed.), *Handbook of Research on Teaching.* (3rd ed.) New York: Macmillan, 1986.

Conti, G. J. "The Relationship Between Teaching Style and Adult Student Learning." *Adult Education Quarterly,* 1985, *35* (4), 220–228.

Copa, P. M., and Sandmann, L. R. "Profile of Excellence: What Makes an Exemplary Professional?" *Journal of Extension,* Fall 1987, pp. 117–124.

Daloz, L. A. *Effective Teaching and Mentoring: Realizing the Transformational Power of Adult Learning Experiences.* San Francisco: Jossey-Bass, 1986.

Dickinson, G. *Teaching Adults: A Handbook for Instructors.* Toronto: New Press, 1973.

Dickinson, G. (ed.). *Introduction to Teaching Adults: Guidelines for Teachers of Adults.* Victoria, British Columbia: Ministry of Education, 1981.

Draves, W. A. *How to Teach Adults.* Manhattan, Kan.: Learning Resources Network, 1984.

Entwistle, N. (ed.). *New Directions in Educational Psychology 1: Learning and Teaching.* London: Falmer Press, 1985.

Fenstermacher, G. D. "A Philosophical Consideration of Recent Research on Teacher Effectiveness." In L. Shulman (ed.), *Review of Research in Education*. Vol. 6. Itasca, Ill.: American Educational Research Association, 1978.

Giroux, H. A., and McLaren, P. "Teacher Education and the Politics of Engagement: The Case for Democratic Schooling." *Harvard Educational Review*, 1986, *56* (3), 213–238.

Greene, M. "In Search of a Critical Pedagogy." *Harvard Educational Review*, 1986, *56* (4), 427–441.

Grimmett, P. P., and Erickson, G. L. (eds.). *Reflection in Teacher Education*. New York: Teachers College Press, 1988.

Guilbert, J. J. *Educational Handbook for Health Personnel*. (Rev. ed.) Geneva: World Health Organization, 1981.

Halkes, R., and Olson, J. K. *Teacher Thinking: A New Perspective on Persisting Problems in Education*. Tilburg, The Netherlands: Lisse, Swets, and Zeitlinger, 1984.

Knowles, M. S. *The Modern Practice of Adult Education*. (2nd ed.) New York: Cambridge Books, 1980.

Lather, P. "Research as Praxis." *Harvard Educational Review*, 1986, *56* (3), 257–277.

Lowman, J. *Mastering the Techniques of Teaching*. San Francisco: Jossey-Bass, 1984.

Marton, F., Hounsell, D., and Entwistle, N. *The Experience of Learning*. Edinburgh: Scottish Academic Press, 1984.

Mezirow, J. D. "A Critical Theory of Adult Learning and Education." *Adult Education*, 1981, *31* (1), 3–24.

Practical Management Associates. *How to Teach Grown-ups*. Canoga Park, Calif.: Practical Management, 1979.

Pratt, D. D. "Teacher Effectiveness—Future Directions for Adult Education." *Studies in Adult Education*, 1981, *13* (2), 112–119.

Pratt, D. D. "Teaching Adults: A Conceptual Framework for the First Session." *Lifelong Learning: An Omnibus of Practice and Research*, 1984, 7 (3), 138–152.

Pratt, D. D. "Technology and Instructional Functions." In J. A. Niemi and D. D. Gooler (eds.), *Technologies for Learning Outside the Classroom*. New Directions for Continuing Education, no. 34. San Francisco: Jossey-Bass, 1987.

Pratt, D. D. "Andragogy as a Relational Construct." *Adult Education Quarterly*, 1988, *38* (3), 160–172.

Renner, P. F. *The Instructor's Survival Kit: A Handbook for Teachers of Adults*. (2nd ed.) Vancouver, British Columbia: Training Associates, 1983.

Rosenshine, B., and Stevens, R. "Teaching Functions." In M. C. Wittrock (ed.), *Handbook of Research on Teaching*. (3rd ed.) New York: Macmillan, 1986.

Schneider-Fuhrmann, B., and Grasha, A. F. *A Practical Handbook for College Teachers*. Toronto: Little, Brown, 1983.

Schön, D. A. *The Reflective Practitioner: How Professionals Think in Action*. New York: Basic Books, 1983.

Shor, I. "Equality Is Excellence: Transforming Teacher Education and the Learning Process." *Harvard Educational Review*, 1986, *56* (4), 406–426.

Shores, W. L. "Study of Interactions of Adult Learners with Learning Situations." Unpublished doctoral dissertation, University of British Columbia, 1985.

Shulman, L. S. "Knowledge and Teaching: Foundations of the New Reform. *Harvard Educational Review*, 1987, *57* (1), 1–22.

Stephens, M. D., and Roderick, G. W. (eds.) *Teaching Techniques in Adult Education*. London: David & Charles, 1974.

Sullivan, B. *Teaching Improvement Project Systems for Health Care Education.* Lexington, Ky.: Center for Learning Resources, no date.

van Manen, M. "Reflections on Teacher Competence and Pedagogic Competence." In E. C. Short (ed.), *Competence: Inquiries into Its Meaning and Acquisition in Educational Settings.* Lanham, Md.: University Press of America, 1984.

Wilson, S. M., Shulman, L. S., and Richert, A. "150 Different Ways of Knowing: Representations of Knowledge in Teaching." In J. Calderhead (ed.), *Exploring Teachers' Thinking.* London: Cassell Educational, 1987.

Daniel D. Pratt is assistant professor of Adult Education at The University of British Columbia. His primary academic interests are adult learning and instruction.

Some concluding thoughts are offered on effective teaching styles and available resources.

Additional Resources for Enhancing Your Personal Style

Elisabeth Hayes, Yvonne A. Petrella

As the education of adults continues to gain importance in many settings, there has been a corresponding concern for the improvement of teaching practices with adult students. The chapters in this volume highlight only a few topics of recent and ongoing significance for teachers of adults.

Teaching is a highly complex activity that requires multiple skills. While this point may seem obvious, too often teachers at every level are not given the recognition or respect that they deserve for the expertise that is needed to do their jobs well. Further, teachers themselves may not be sensitive to the many elements that contribute to the success or failure of their teaching efforts.

While the authors in this volume address a variety of issues, a common theme is the need for greater teacher self-awareness as a first step for the improvement of teaching in continuing education. As the research discussed by Darkenwald in Chapter Six reveals, teachers' perceptions of various aspects of the adult classroom situation, including their own behavior, can be very different from the perceptions of their students. Becoming more aware of what we are doing as teachers and of our impact on students provides the opportunity for reflection on the reasons for

E. R. Hayes (ed.). *Effective Teaching Styles.*
New Directions for Continuing Education, no. 43. San Francisco: Jossey-Bass, Fall 1989.

these actions. Are we merely reacting to situational demands, or do we make a deliberate attempt to develop a teaching style based on explicit values and assumptions, as advocated by Apps in Chapter Two and by Conti in Chapter One? Do we let such factors as available technology control the teaching process, or do we follow the adjuration of Florini in Chapter Four and ensure that technology is used to serve our own clearly defined goals?

The current acknowledgement—implicit or explicit in all chapters—that there is not a single model of effective teaching for adults makes such suggestions of particular importance. Theories of teaching and learning, such as andragogy, offer but single approaches that may be more or less effective given a variety of variables. Without a clear-cut formula to follow, it becomes much more critical for teachers to be able to make informed decisions about their own practice.

In Chapter Three, Bonham suggests benefits of reflection on teaching practices that extend beyond the selection and mastery of appropriate instructional strategies. This attention to the teaching process reinforces and reflects less definable aspects of positive teaching style—the enthusiasm and concern that are cited time after time as characteristics of motivating, memorable, influential teachers. As Pratt notes in Chapter Seven, professional development involves an ongoing process of expanding and enhancing our notions of competent teaching. Seeing the opportunity in each new teaching experience for our own continued learning and growth enables us to maintain the excitement and interest in teaching that is transferred so contagiously to our students.

Professional growth demands a continual consideration of multiple perspectives on desirable goals and strategies for the teaching process. One way to broaden our own perspectives is to seek out the experiences and ideas of others. Thus, it seems appropriate to end this volume with a list of resources that adult educators can use to continue their process of professional development. While there is a wide array of material on various aspects of teaching adults, there is very little that focuses specifically on teaching styles. Therefore, resources have been selected from the wider body of literature. Both more recent and classic works have been included. As Pratt notes, at each stage of professional development what was previously taken for granted can become an object of new concern; thus, even if some sources are already familiar, they may yield new insights when read again from another perspective.

With a few exceptions, only books have been included here. Many journal articles may also be valuable. The journals published by such professional groups as the American Association for Adult and Continuing Education (AAACE), the Association for Continuing Higher Education (ACHE), and the American Society for Training and Development (ASTD) include helpful information related to teaching styles. The list in this chapter is by no means exhaustive; instead, it is a selective representation of diverse perspectives and approaches to teaching adults. Our comments indicate the general orientation of each resource and particular highlights.

Selected Resources

Apps, Jerold W. *Higher Education in a Learning Society: Meeting New Demands for Education and Training.* San Francisco: Jossey-Bass, 1988.

Educational institutions face new challenges as the next decade approaches. In order to respond to those challenges, many institutions will need to change their structure and broaden their mission. Apps provides ways of planning for changes and meeting the curriculum needs of learners. In Chapter Seven, he cites uses of educational technology as a way of diversifying the approaches to instruction. Chapter Eleven examines the changing role of the faculty, factors that contribute to faculty resistance to change, and strategies to influence change. Administrators will find Chapter Eleven helpful for suggestions on facilitating change to assist teachers in becoming more effective.

Brookfield, Stephen D. *Developing Critical Thinkers: Challenging Adults to Explore Alternative Ways of Thinking and Acting.* San Francisco: Jossey-Bass, 1987.

The premise of Brookfield's book is that the value of critical thinking goes beyond the traditional classroom and is useful in various aspects of adult life as it relates to the workplace, politics, and learning. Part Two, "Practical Approaches for Developing Critical Thinkers," includes a chapter on strategies for facilitating critical thinking, which provides several ways for the instructor to facilitate critical thinking. In Chapter Twelve, Brookfield focuses on how to be a skilled facilitator of critical thinking.

Brookfield, Stephen D. *Understanding and Facilitating Adult Learning: A Comprehensive Analysis of Principles and Effective Practices.* San Francisco: Jossey-Bass, 1986.

As the title states, Brookfield provides a review of the principles of adult learning and suggestions for teachers to facilitate the learning process of adults. Brookfield also examines adults' motives for learning. He explains the concepts of self-directed learning and suggests ways for instructors to facilitate the self-directed learning process. Included in the book is a discussion on developing and structuring programs around learners' needs. He suggests that the facilitator is a practical theorist, one who implements theory effectively in teaching and in program development.

Cranton, Patricia. *Planning Instruction for Adult Learners.* Toronto: Wall & Thompson, 1989.

Cranton introduces the reader to theories of learning and suggests ways of using them to develop instruction. Two chapters that will be useful to new teachers are "Developing the Instructional Strategy" and "Evaluating Learning". The first is especially useful, as it contains several tables matching strategy to situation and group size.

Daloz, Laurent A. *Effective Teaching and Mentoring: Realizing the Transformational Power of Adult Learning Experiences.* San Francisco: Jossey-Bass, 1986.

Using the metaphor of a journey, Daloz shares his experiences as a mentor of adult students through case studies and reflections of his own experiences. Early chapters explain the concept of mentoring and the roles that it can include. Later chapters focus on the learner's process of growth and transformation. Daloz's major point is that the learning process is not an end but a means to growth.

Draves, William A. *How to Teach Adults.* Manhattan, Kansas: Learning Resources Network, 1984.

In this full-length book, Draves provides more detailed information on how adults learn and suggests several ways for the instructor to facilitate the learning process. Included is a chapter on how to prepare course objectives, determine structure, and gauge the amount of material to be covered. In addition to offering suggestions for teaching techniques, Draves also discusses ways of involving participants. There is also a short chapter on preparing for the first class.

Draves, William A. *How to Teach Adults in One Hour.* Manhattan, Kansas: Learning Resources Network, 1988.

This booklet provides a clear, concise, and practical overview of techniques for teaching adults. It includes suggestions for the new instructor about how to prepare and create the proper learning environment. This short handbook is especially helpful for educators who are new to working with adults or technicians who will be offering training sessions.

Eble, Kenneth E. *The Aims of College Teaching.* San Francisco: Jossey-Bass, 1983.

The focus of Eble's book is on developing a personal teaching style and recognizing the impact that an instructor's teaching style has on the student and the learning process. He suggests ways of developing and using senior faculty members as mentors for new teachers. While Eble's focus is on college teaching, adult educators will find that his ideas are easily applied to adult learning situations. Chapter Seven addresses the characteristics of ineffective teaching and how to avoid such situations.

Ingalls, John D. *A Trainer's Guide to Andragogy.* Washington, D.C.: U.S. Department of Health, Education, and Welfare, 1973.

This practical guide opens with a chapter explaining the concept of andragogy that provides the foundation for the rest of the book. Included is information on forming educational and training objectives, applying the concepts of andragogy to teaching and learning, and ways of designing and implementing adult learning activities. Ingalls also provides trainers with worksheets and experiential exercises for their own use.

Knowles, Malcolm. *Self-Directed Learning: A Guide for Learners and Teachers.* New York: Association Press, 1975.

Using his own experiences as examples, Knowles discusses the instructor's role as a facilitator and ways of promoting self-directed learning in the context of a classroom. The book includes samples of resources that can be used to implement the principles of self-directed learning, such as instruments with which students can rate their competency levels, learning contracts, relationship-building exercises, and student self-assessment exercises. Knowles includes a discussion of learning contracts and how to use them to facilitate the student's learning process.

Knox, Alan B. *Helping Adults Learn: A Guide to Planning, Implementing, and Conducting Programs.* San Francisco: Jossey-Bass, 1986.

Knox provides an overview of the factors to consider in developing effective and useful programs for adults. Topics range from needs assessment, sequencing activities, evaluation, and available materials to support instruction. Also included is a chapter that examines the many ways in which an instructor can assist participants in applying what is learned.

Mager, Robert F., *Preparing Instructional Objectives.* Belmont, California: Fearon, 1975.

Mager presents his ideas on developing instructional objectives in an interactive style. The reader is an active participant in asking and responding to questions. The reader's responses guide her or him through the various processes of identifying and developing various types of objectives. Mager stresses the value of writing clear objectives so that the students know what is expected of them. He also includes a chapter on how to develop criteria to evaluate performance.

National Center for Research in Vocational Education, *Category N— Teaching Adults* (6 modules). Athens, Georgia: American Association for Vocational Instructional Materials, 1987.

This series of workbooks offers brief discussions of a variety of topics ranging from marketing and needs assessment to planning and implementing adult instruction and evaluating performance. Each module presents information on a selected topic along with exercises, checklists, and a listing of other resources. The titles of the six modules are as follows:

Prepare to Work with Adults (N-1)
Market an Adult Education Program (N-2)
Determine the Individual Training Needs (N-3)
Plan Instruction for Adults (N-4)
Manage the Adult Instructional Process (N-5)
Evaluate the Performance of Adults (N-6)

New Directions for Continuing Education. San Francisco: Jossey-Bass.

The volumes in this series of quarterly sourcebooks cover a wide range of topics of interest to instructors and administrators in the field of adult and continuing education. Several focus on such issues as teaching adults, selecting and developing instructional materials, and ways of involving adults in the learning process. Volumes of particular relevance for the improvement of instruction include: *Attracting Able Instructors of Adults* (no. 4), *Teaching Adults Effectively* (no. 6), *Materials for Teaching Adults: Selection, Development, and Use* (no. 17), *Helping Adults Learn How to Learn* (no. 19), *Involving Adults in the Educational Process* (no. 26), and *Experiential and Simulation Techniques for Teaching Adults* (no. 30).

New Directions for Teaching and Learning. San Francisco: Jossey-Bass.

This series of quarterly sourcebooks focuses on college teaching, but a number of volumes are relevant for educators in many settings. In each volume, experts and practitioners address current and significant issues in teaching with suggestions of new techniques, state-of-the-art resources, and ways of solving common classroom problems. Particularly useful volumes include *Improving Teaching Styles* (no. 1), *Learning About Teaching* (no. 4), *Expanding Learning Through New Communications Technologies* (no. 9), *Learning in Groups* (no. 14), *Teaching Minority Students* (no. 16), *Developing Critical Thinking and Problem-Solving Abilities* (no. 30), and *Teaching Large Classes Well* (no. 32).

Rogers, Alan. *Teaching Adults.* Philadelphia: Open University Press, 1986.

Early chapters of Rogers' book focus on learning theories and on setting goals and objectives. He includes a chapter on the role of the teacher and suggestions of ways to teach adults. Later chapters examine blocks to learning and the need for evaluation and participation in the adult learning process.

Rogers, Carl R. *Freedom to Learn for the '80s.* (Rev. ed.) Columbus, Ohio: Merrill, 1983.

In the revised edition of this classic, Rogers offers ways for educators to interact with learners effectively and create a climate for learning. A reflection of his personal philosophy, this book is also a reflection of humanist thought. Rogers addresses the fallacies of traditional educational thinking, demonstrates the value of learner-centered education, and discusses the consequences when learners do not take control or have the "freedom to learn."

Schön, Donald A. *Educating the Reflective Practitioner: Toward a New Design for Teaching and Learning in the Profession.* San Francisco: Jossey-Bass, 1987.

Schön's premise is that the practitioner needs to reflect upon theory and action in order to make decisions in a world where issues and decisions cannot always be easily categorized. Using examples of studio-related subjects from art and music, Schön discusses ways for professionals to teach their craft. One chapter that may be of particular interest examines the issues that result when teaching and learning do not create the desired outcome. Schön also discusses how a reflective practicum can bridge the gap between the university and practice.

Seaman, Don F., and Fellenz, Robert A. *Effective Strategies for Teaching Adults.* Columbus, Ohio: Merrill, 1989.

Seaman and Fellenz provide a concise guide for practitioners in continuing education. Their book describes a number of strategies for teaching adults, such as learning teams, dialogues, and debates, and examines their strengths and weaknesses. Each section also includes suggested uses of each strategy in different situations. A valuable chapter on evaluating teaching effectiveness is included, which new and experienced instructors will find helpful.

Shor, Ira. *Critical Teaching and Everyday Life.* Boston: South End Press, 1980.

This book offers one of the few detailed discussions of the application of Freire's radical educational ideas in a North American setting. Shor's concrete description of teaching strategies that he used with working-class adult students in a community college program is a valuable model for teachers interested in this approach.

Tom, Alan R. *Teaching as a Moral Craft.* New York: Longman, 1984.

Tom addresses the problems of viewing teaching as an applied science and concludes that there really is no one best way to teach. He also presents an overview of the research on effective teaching behavior and the faulty assumptions underlying much of that research. One chapter examines the moral dimension of student-teacher relationships and the teacher's moral responsibility for the development of another individual. A chapter on the craft basis of teaching discusses the value of experience, applying knowledge to specific situations, and teaching as an intellectually based activity.

Wlodkowski, Raymond J. *Enhancing Adult Motivation to Learn: A Guide to Improving Instruction and Increasing Learner Achievement.* San Francisco: Jossey-Bass, 1986.

The major thrust of Wlodkowski's book is the importance of motivation in the learning process and its effect on instruction. In addition to discussing the characteristics and skills of a motivating instructor, he also includes strategies for helping adults develop positive attitudes and strategies for making learning stimulating. A chapter on incorporating motivation into the instructional plan is especially helpful. This chapter also includes a self-evaluation plan for instructors and a summary table of motivational strategies. Overall, this book provides useful strategies for both new and experienced teachers.

Elisabeth Hayes is assistant professor of adult education at Syracuse University.

Yvonne A. Petrella is a member of the faculty at the State University of New York, College at Oswego, where she teaches marketing.

Index

A

Adult Classroom Environment Scale (ACES), 69–74; benefits of using, 74; dimensions and subscales, 72; items, 69–71; profiles for, 73; research findings of, 69, 72–74
Adults as learners, 20–27
Alley, R., 36, 40
American Association for Adult and Continuing Education (AAACE), 90
American Society for Training and Development (ASTD), 90
Andragogy, 90, 93
Aoki, T., 82–83, 85
Apple, M. W., 83, 85
Apps, J. W., 18–19, 27, 91
Aptitude-treatment interaction, 34
Arterton, F. C., 50, 53
Ary, D., 34, 39
Association for Continuing Higher Education (ACHE), 90

B

Baker-Miller, J. B., 56, 65
Beder, H. W., 5–6, 15
Belenky, M. F., 55, 56–57, 65
Bem, D., 17, 27
Berliner, D. C., 81, 85
Berry, E., 61–62, 65
Berry, W., 19, 27
Black, E., 61–62, 65
Bloom, B. S., 5, 15, 78, 85
Bonham, L. A., 35, 39
Boud, D., 22, 27
Brand, S., 42, 53
Brookfield, S. D., 4–5, 16, 81, 83, 85, 91
Brophy, J., 80, 85
Bunch, C., 59, 62–63, 65

C

Calderhead, J., 81, 85
Canfield, A. A., 4, 16, 30–31, 39

Canfield, J. S., 4, 16, 30, 39
Canfield Instructional Styles Inventory, 30
Canfield Learning Styles Inventory, 30, 35–36
Carlson, D., 83, 85
Carnegie Foundation for the Advancement of Teaching, 48–49
Charlton, R. E., 34, 39
Clark, C., 79, 85
Classroom environment: and ACES, 69–74; concept of, 67–68; enhancing, 67–75; measuring, 68–69; and teaching styles, 68
Classroom Environment Scale (CES), 69
Claxton, C. S., 30, 39
Clinchy, B. M., 55, 56–57, 65
Coates, J., 57, 65
Cognitive Style Interest Inventory, 31
Collaborative learning, 59–61
Compton, J. L., 24, 27
Computer conferencing, 43–45, 51
Computer-assisted interactive video (CAIV), 43–45, 50
Consciousness-raising groups, 61
Content knowledge, defined, 78
Conti, G. J., 11–13, 16, 81, 85
Continuing education, teaching style and, 3–16
Copa, P. M., 80, 85
Cox, P. W., 30, 31, 40
Cranton, P., 92
Critical thinking, 81–85, 91
Cronbach, L. J., 34, 39

D

Daloz, L. A., 5, 16, 81, 85, 92
Darkenwald, G. G., 4–6, 15, 16, 69, 74
Davidman, L., 36, 39
DeLoughry, T. J., 48–49, 53
Dickinson, G., 79, 85
Donnelly, W. J., 42, 53
Doyle, W., 34, 39
Draves, W. A., 79, 85, 92